WORKDAY CHRISTIANITY.

WORKDAY CHRISTIANITY:

OR,

THE GOSPEL IN THE TRADES.

BY

ALEXANDER CLARK,

AUTHOR OF "THE GOSPEL IN THE TREES," "THE OLD LOG SCHOOLHOUSE," ETC.

WITH AN INTRODUCTORY NOTE

BY WILLIAM CULLEN BRYANT.

PHILADELPHIA:
CLAXTON, REMSEN & HAFFELFINGER,
819 & 821 MARKET STREET.
SPRINGFIELD, OHIO: METHODIST PUBLISHING HOUSE.
PITTSBURGH: S. A. CLARKE & CO.
1871.

STEREOTYPED BY J. FAGAN & SON. PRINTED BY MOORE BROTHERS.

Dedication.

TO

THOMAS W. SHAW, M. D.,
JAMES S. ATTERBURY,
SAMUEL WILLIAMS,
WILLIAM J. TROTH,

OF THE CONGREGATION WHERE HE HAS WORSHIPED;

AND TO

DANIEL SCHINDLER AND J. C. HARPER,

OF THE PITTSBURGH PRESS,—

This Volume

IS RESPECTFULLY DEDICATED,

IN GRATEFUL REMEMBRANCE OF KIND AND APPROVING WORDS,

WHEN ENCOURAGEMENT IN HIS WORK

WAS ESPECIALLY NEEDED,—

BY THE AUTHOR.

INTRODUCTORY NOTE.

HAVE read "Workday Christianity," and have been pleased with the ingenuity with which the author illustrates religious truths by things which correspond with them in the material world, especially by the methods and processes of the mechanic arts. The work will, I think, do good.

I particularly like the catholic spirit which pervades these pages, and the superiority to mere dogmatical distinctions which they show, accounting him to be a true Christian, whatever his sect, who is a sincere follower of Jesus Christ, and faithfully obeys the law of love which he taught.

The style is clear and well suited to the subjects.

W. C. BRYANT.

NEW YORK, *March* 16, 1870.

	Page
I.	
The Carpenter	11
II.	
The Mason	33
III.	
The Bricklayer	57
IV.	
The Founder	81
V.	
The Machinist	111
VI.	
The Potter	137

VII.

PAGE

THE GLASSMAKER 163

VIII.

THE PILOT 191

IX.

THE PRINTER 217

X.

THE WEAVER 243

XI.

THE DAY-LABORER 267

THE CARPENTER.

"Is not this the Carpenter?"—MARK vi. 3.

WORKDAY CHRISTIANITY.

CHAPTER I.

THE CARPENTER.

THE first sentence of Holy Scripture reveals God as a Creator. He created the heavens and the earth. The wondrous fabric was not formed by any fortuitous circumstances. There was a design, outwrought by a beginning, a process, and a consummation. The statement is distinct and absolute. A Supreme Intelligence moulded and furnitured the world, and recorded the great fact as first in the order of revelation. The entire Bible maintains the doctrine of creation as the work of an independent and an almighty Person, and emphasizes it to all generations of people, that it may never pass from mind, by fixing upon one day in every seven as a commemoration of the finished work. Every Sabbath's sun is a celestial seal set to the truth written in the first chapter of Genesis. The orrery of the universe is but a clock to mark the coming of the hallowed day of rest.

The Bible shows us also, as a whole, by both its former and its latter testimonies, that He who made the world "in the beginning," condescended, "in the fullness of time," to suffering and sorrow amidst its scenes, to redeem and reconstruct that portion which sin had ruined. How fitting that He who created should repair! Creation and Redemption are the accordant octave-tones that reverberate through all the Bible from the Alpha of Genesis to the Omega of Revelation — whose music echoes forever from earth to heaven and from heaven to earth. The infinite Word and the infinite Work are unifold. The Creator and the Redeemer are one. The power that built and the power that restores are the same. "In the beginning was the Word, and the

Word was with God, and the Word was God. The same was in the beginning with God. All things were made by Him; and without Him was not anything made that was made. . . . And the Word was made flesh, and dwelt among us. . . . He was in the world, and the world was made by Him, and the world knew Him not."

For there was a wide distance between the gate of Eden and the cradle of Bethlehem. There was a lapse of forty centuries from the time when God talked with Adam in Paradise, until he worked with Joseph as a carpenter. The infinite wisdom that planned and framed a universe of worlds, was not in haste in rounding out the fullness of time when Messiah should appear.

Never is the divine method necessarily splendid, startling, or imposing in its operations. The great era of creation was finished before the eyes of men were opened to behold. The procedures were not for exhibition. It is enough for human intelligence to witness results when Omnipotence works. The ways of God are past finding out. Behind his most stupendous operations, and in the execution of his grandest plans, there is "a hiding of his power." The material universe came into existence without attesting human witnesses, to stand as a self-evident fact; and so, evermore, "the kingdom of God cometh not with observation."

Men, themselves the creatures of dust, are apt to speak of storms, of volcanoes, of earthquakes, of convulsions and of revolutions — to make a noise and stir to attract attention; but God speaks in "the still, small voice." Hence the people are slow to believe the statement of Moses in reference to the creation, and the account of the evangelists in reference to redemption. That such great things should be so simply said and so quietly done, is an evidence of divinity that babbling mortals can not apprehend. They are not prepared to accept a Saviour in the person of a carpenter. Nazareth is too near home to rear a prophet. Men would naturally expect a triumphal descent from heaven, an angel convoy with bugles to rouse the masses, chariots and horses of fire, a magnificent royal advent of the Messiah robed in glory and radiant with light — a kingly coming that should strike the nations with amazement, and compel, by physical powers, the allegiance of the people.

But that the Son of God should appear as a babe, be announced to a few poor shepherds in the fields by night, be obscured for tedious years as the son of a carpenter, and wear the form and show the tan and brusqueness of a servant — this was beneath belief! Mary, the mother of Jesus, was neither a ruler nor a ruler's daughter. She was of David's line, a royal ancestry, to be sure; but her immediate relatives were humble and retired. Her husband was a mechanic. As a family, their circumstances were limited, for as the birth-offering of their firstborn, a lamb could not be afforded, and a pair of turtle doves, the pledge that poverty presents, were the consecrating sacrifice when the child Jesus was given to the Lord in the solemn temple service. He was brought up to habits of industry, economy and self-denial, in Nazareth. His hands were hardened by daily toil. He put his shoulder to heavy timbers, drove the saw and plane, and swung the hammer in honest work. It was not considered a disgrace in those days to ply a trade. Even the Rabbins were accustomed to some handicraft. There is a tradition that Jesus constructed plows and farming utensils, as well as the articles of common carpentry. Paul was a tent-maker, and nearly all the apostles were tradesmen. None of them were above work. Some of them were used to drudging toil. It would seem that employment, from the morning of creation, when God himself worked and rested, and when Adam was commanded to till the soil and subdue the animals, implies peculiar dignity and honor. The Maker of worlds blesses labor. It is apostolic, it is Christ-like, it is God-like to work. No system of education is complete that does not harden the hand and toughen the muscle, while it develops the intellect and enlarges the heart. The religion that shows nothing but pale cheeks and lily-white fingers is not the religion of the Bible. Highways and hedges are better sanctuaries for acceptable service, than studies, and cloisters, and cells. Scars and knots on the hands are more honorable than rings and gloves. Bronze out of the sunbeams is more beautiful on the face than rouge out of the shops. Only a worker attains the true symmetry, strength and glory of manhood or womanhood. Genius itself falters in a conflict with labor. Industry has the long end of the lever that moves public opinions, parties, congresses, and thrones. It was men with brown faces and sinewy arms that built the pyramids on Egypt's plains, reared the temple on Mount Moriah, and walled the Holy City with adamant, circled an Asiatic Empire with impenetrable granite, put arm in arm the old and the new worlds as whispering mother and daughter, spanned the American continent with a thoroughfare of iron from sea to sea, cut a canal for steamers in forty months across the desert sands where the Israelites wandered for forty years; it is men with sunburnt features and nerves of steel that to-day whiten the world's wide waters with the sails of commerce, navigate all rivers, explore all lands, subdue the earth as God at first commanded. An idle man, however white, and soft, and smart, is not God's man!

But the people of Nazareth, near twenty centuries ago, were very like the people of larger cities now. They heard the wonderful words of Jesus, and were astonished. But their surprise gave place to jealousy and indignation. "Is not this the carpenter, the son of Mary, the brother of James and Joses, and of Juda and Simon, and are not his sisters here with us? And they were offended in him." As much as to say, "We know his family and his standing in society. He is but a mechanic, the son of a mechanic, one of the common people, one of our poor neighbors, a hewer of wood, an obscure tradesman of Nazareth!" But what an unintended tribute of respect is this! The Son of God was the Son of Man. He grew up to human maturity amid toils and tears, eating the bread of manual labor every day, and resting as a wearied worker every night. He mingled with the people, not as a guest, or stranger, or superior, for all these thirty years; but as with his fellow-beings, as one of themselves, engaged in active industry, and known as an ordinary mechanic. There are fastidious professors of his religion now, who would scarcely have stooped to enter his shop among the chips and shavings, or to have taken his homely hand in their delicate grasp, or to have eaten at the same table with the hungry Nazarene! To some stylish Christians, in these modern times, fingers are only intended for twirling a cane, for folding away mortgages, for lifting to dainty lips domestic wines, for pointing out the broad acres of estate and its high stories of mansion which men call their own. Some men who were once common laborers, made rich by smiling Providences and the hard knocks of busy hands, have children who turn away in scorn from the mechanic and the laborer. It is astonishing to see how soon the homely phrases of industry and the Frenchy words of fashion exchange places in the vocabulary of some people. There is a well turned truth in the familiar lines remembered from schooldays:

"One day, a rich man, flushed with pride and wine,
Sitting with guests at table, all quite merry,
Conceived it would be vastly fine
To crack a joke upon his secretary.

'Young man,' said he, 'by what art, craft or trade,
Did your good father earn his livelihood?'
'He was a saddler, sir,' the young man said,
'And, in his line, was reckoned very good.'
'A saddler, eh? and had you stuffed with Greek,
Instead of teaching you like him to do!
And pray, sir, why did not your father make
A saddler, too, of you?'
At this each flatterer, as in duty bound,
The joke applauded, and the laugh went round.

"At length, the secretary, bending low,
Said, (craving pardon if too free he made,)
'Sir, by your leave, I fain would know
Your father's trade?'
'*My* father's *trade?* Why, sir, but that 's too bad!
My father's trade! Why, blockhead, art thou mad?
My father, sir, was never brought so low;
He was a *gentleman*, I 'd have you know!'
'Indeed! excuse the liberty I take;
But, if the story 's true,
How happened it your father did not make
A gentleman of you!'"

True gentility as well as true genius is oftenest found among the common people, made healthy and happy by willing work. Profess in science what you may; cling to whatever social clan you choose; accept for religion nothing but ceremony and cadence if you will; pity the plain, plodding mechanic if you must; but remember withal, that the Lord of glory was a carpenter! Those hands which touched the cripple, and made him leap for joy; the dumb, and turned his tongue to praise; the deaf, and charmed his ears with melody; the dead, and brought him back to life; those hands that rested in benedictions on little children's heads; that fed the hungry multitudes; that grasped and held still the furious tempest of the sea; that were nailed to the rough timber of the cross; those hands for many years were skilled in the use of the axe, the adze, and the plane. How passing strange that the hearts of fellow countrymen should conspire against him, and that the hands of fellow craftsmen should frame the wood on which he was crucified!

The people were not ready to accept the teachings of a tradesman as the words of a prophet. They were looking in another direction for truth; they expected something more august, regal, and outwardly magnificent. And to this day, there are thousands in Christendom who reject the gospel because it is so simple and familiar in its manner. They fail to apprehend the divinity that wears so plain a garb. They fashion gaudy garments for the Divine word. They supplement the Bible by ritual, dogma, or creed—by councils, theologies, and views — until "the faith once delivered to the saints" is lost in the verbiage of the sect, instead of held in the life of the soul. The heavenliest principle in the gospel is its manifested love in Jesus Christ, who, "being in the form of God, thought it not robbery to be equal with God; but made himself of no reputation, and took upon himself the form of a servant, and was made in the likeness of men." Yes, indeed, he completely assumed our nature, accepting its toil, its care, its weariness, its hunger, its thirst, its sweat, its suffering, its shame — everything but its sin. It would have been great condescension for God's Son to assume an earthly throne and to make himself brother to kings and level with carnal conquerors. But he did more: he became the apprentice of a mechanic, and endured years of toil as equal of the workingman, while really the Master and Redeemer of all.

There is, also, a lesson of patience in this. There were some ten years of matured physical manhood spent in manual labor at the bench. Enthusiasts would call that wasted time — years wrested from his special mission in the world. Young men must be hurried into the ministry now, at twenty. The church's loudest calls to-day are for pastors on the sunny side of thirty. Precocious preachers command a premium in the market. But "God's ways are not as our ways, nor His thoughts as our thoughts." He never needs to be in haste. He works out his designs by the fullnesses of time. The Eternal is not guided by clock or calendar. Many men become restless, uneasy, and even violent to attempt and accomplish certain schemes. The heart sometimes leaps forward, when the head says, "Hold; be calm; keep still." For always there must be wisdom to balance impulse, and discretion to parallel devotion.

Christians are often rash in their methods to extend the Redeemer's kingdom. They go by feeling rather than by faith. There must be growths in grace; not fits and starts, but steady increase. Growth in grace is the only clear gain. No winter overtakes it. It is perennial. Sometimes churches will engage in what they presumptuously announce beforehand as a "revival work." They who pretend to be shocked at the advertising of special gospel themes from the human side, will venture to advertise "revival," which is the peculiar work of God! They will press every force into an effort of a few days, neglecting family, business, everything else, attempting to condense into the convenient focus of a week the opportunities and agencies of a whole round year, deliberately unsettling health of body for the sake of souls. Great results are programmed for a certain convenient time. God must serve in seasons set by men, and according to the methods made sectarian by men. Then, the excitement ended, the half a hundred and one other weeks lapse into a dullness and dumbness which even the secular world might pity. There is never a necessity for spasmodic strains or pyrotechnic exhibitions in Christian work;

but always a necessity for earnest, practical, honest, persistent action in rescuing men from sin. The true revival spirit is "instant in season and out of season," is always alert and active, and claims the summer noon as well as the winter midnight as the set time to favor Zion. The gospel is good news in seed-time and in harvest; out in the field among the shepherds, at the river side among the purple-sellers, on the mountain, on the sea, at the wedding, at the funeral, at home, or in the sanctuary. It is like its divine Author, "the same yesterday, and to-day, and forever." It has all times for its own. Christ never showed impatience nor confused haste in his ministries. He was always deliberate, tender, persuasive, and O, how compassionate!—but calm, firm, and orderly in his dealings with sinners, recognizing and honoring the physical, mental and social interests of the people, while specially pleading for the souls of all. Hence, his fewer words were spoken with a power that remained. He addressed men as intelligent beings, hingeing salvation on the human will. He presented religion, not as a system of thought, or an impulse of the heart, but as a believing and consecrated life. The truth that he *preached* he *was!* The gospel that he proclaimed touched and blest men in their places and in their work. He spent the round of laborious years as a carpenter, and did not begin his public ministry until the full-bearded maturity of thirty. Is there not a lesson of patience and deliberate method in this?

The fact that our Saviour was a mechanic is an effectual argument against the popular delusion that greatness is leveled by birth, rank, or wealth. There is no such thing as caste or aristocracy among the angels. They are as willing to watch in a lonely grave as to sing in the open sky. They do not feel humiliated in stepping to the lowest round of the ladder that rests in the dark wilderness, nor elated when they soar about the eternal throne. They shout the same exultant strains when a new world is made and when a lonely wanderer in this repents and turns to God. It is said of Peter the Great, the Czar of Russia, that, in order to familiarize himself with ship-building, he disguised himself and entered the Dutch village of Saardam, and for some time labored as a common workman, under the assumed name of Peter Michaeloff. He was well called Peter the Great, even if for no other act than that. It is great to be humble. It is greater for a ruler to get down than for a subject to get up. One of the greatest things that Abraham Lincoln did while President, was every morning to black his own boots. The people believe in such men. The Apostle Paul forfeited none of his dignity, when, occasionally, he rested from his public ministrations, and resumed, for a change, his former employment of tent-making. He preferred tent-making to spongeing. So the Saviour evinced real grandeur of person and glory of character, by laboring as a carpenter. The hands that put worlds and suns together as a universe, could put stiles and panels together as a door or gate. The hands that framed the lofty vault of the firmament, and frescoed it with golden stars, could frame the rafters of a poor man's cottage in Nazareth. The hands that laid the crystal floors of the eternal city, and spread them as a sea of glass, could put down the planks of a lowly porch in the hill country of Judea.

Religion does not altogether consist of devotional exercises, but, as well, of daily work. We get a wrong idea of Christianity when we reduce it all to songs and sermons, to prayers, solemn faces and ecclesiastical paraphernalia. It is not especially for Sabbaths and sanctuaries, but also for week days, for shops, for homes, for mills, for stores, for streets and fields. Religion is largely an out-door institution. Its Author was born, baptized, transfigured, and crucified under no roof but the sky. It means diligence in business, serving the Lord in common vocations and everyday relations, as well as in consecrated syllables on set occasions. Jesus was more sublimely great standing unknown by men at the carpenter's bench in Nazareth, with apron on, than if he had been surpliced as a priest in the temple, or arrayed in robes of royalty on Pilate's throne. He was greater with an adze in his hand than with a crown on his head. Christianity allows no aversion toward the mechanic. It gives him honorable position. It invites him to its home, and visits him in his. Yet how many rich young ladies who would scorn to associate with the sons and daughters of our workingmen! The matrimonial problems that busy their brains involve such fractions as lawyers, physicians, large-salaried preachers, wholesale merchants, millionaires, and gentlemen of leisure. It would be ridiculous, they think, to throw themselves away on mechanics! Of course, society has its affinities, and that is well. Education grants it. Refinement and culture always seek their level. But we dig *down* for gold. Too often, dissipated dandyism is petted and honored, while intelligent industry is denied a place. The difference between building houses and selling houses is not so great that one should be considered contemptible and the other illustrious. Really, as a business, it makes but little difference whether a man mends clothes, bones, pens, houses, laws, or morals. Work is work and nothing less; man is man and nothing more. Suppose some of our fastidious churchists had met the journeyman joiner of Nazareth on our streets, would they have nodded to him? Would they have invited him to their parlors? Hearing so practical a preacher say such wonderful things in so plain a way, would they not have said — are there not many imitative aristocrats in republican communities who would now say — "Is not this the carpenter?"

The church of God is no place to carry prejudice against labor. Christ himself stands identified with the toiling poor. He would have all associated discipleship plain and free, to bear no higher title than "The Mechanics' Church" — the church where laborers meet, mingle, love each other, are loved of all, and worship God. During the Saviour's ministry on earth, he preached the gospel through nature, through the trades and occupations of the times — farming, fishing, herding, merchandizing, vine-dressing, building, and the "common people heard him gladly." The Nazarene carpenter has left a religion in the world for the busy masses. It rebukes oppression, fraud, indolence, tinsel, and caste. The rich men and rulers may reject the gospel, but it is glad-tidings to the laboring classes, for it blesses their bodies, develops their minds, and saves their souls. "God hath chosen the poor of this world, rich in faith, and heirs of the kingdom which he hath promised to them that love him." The pure religion and undefiled has been perpetuated through humble families. Reformations have sprung from the pious hearts of common people. The church of Christ owes no favor to the rich and great of the earth; but it has a truly noble and brilliant record in the "short and simple annals of the poor."

"Knowing his deeds of love, men questioned not
The faith of One whose walk and word were right,
Who tranquilly in life's great task-field wrought,
And, side by side with evil, never caught
A stain upon his pilgrim garb of white."

Mechanics and workingmen everywhere, the gospel announces a Saviour at your side. He meets you in your places of toil. He brings salvation to your very doors. The church of Jesus Christ is for you a congenial home. Its fellowship is just what you need. Will you receive the Nazarene carpenter as your companion, and accept him as your God?

THE MASON.

"Behold, I lay in Zion for a foundation a stone, a tried stone, a precious corner-stone, a sure foundation."—ISAIAH xxviii. 16.

CHAPTER II.

THE MASON.

FREQUENTLY the church of God is designated in the Holy Scriptures by the figure of a building, stately, symmetrical, and solid. The apostle Paul, addressing the Ephesian believers, recognizes them as a portion of the compact edifice "built upon the foundation of the apostles and prophets, Jesus Christ himself being the chief corner-stone." The doctrine of redemption, ranging through the Old and the New Testaments — the Messiah of the prophets and the Christ of the apostles — is the one sure and safe foundation. The fact of a Redeemer born, anointed, crucified, buried, risen, and alive forevermore, underlies the whole superstructure of the church. Peter, a preacher of the new dispensation, quoting the prophecy of Isaiah of the old dispensation, says, as warrant for his faith, "Wherefore it is contained in the Scripture, Behold, I lay in Zion a chief corner-stone, elect, precious, and he that believeth on Him shall not be confounded." A corner-stone is the choice and calculated stone that binds two walls and makes them one. It is the seal that holds the broad foundation in solid body as a base. Paul uses the same idea in his language to the Corinthians, "For other foundation can no man lay than is laid, which is Jesus Christ."

The prominent thought in the topic is this: *Christ the foundation of the Church.* It is a figure framed from the facts of common observation. It is so familiar and significant that a child may apprehend it. The prophets and the apostles go to the mason for an illustration. Many of the great truths of God find fittest expression through the facts and forms of ordinary work. The well-known phrase from Shakespeare, "sermons in stones," originates in the Bible. Indeed, the poets and philosophers of all ages, more largely than may be dreamed, gather their best thoughts from the pages of Divine inspiration.

A foundation is a beginning. It may be composed of material older than history. But, set to a corner-stone, it implies purpose, afterwork, and finish. Masonry is the essential body of architecture. It puts in place the imperishable. It holds its records in granite and marble. Its registries are ancient and royal. However near the Eden-gate its first design may have been wrought into form, one of its earliest monuments was that of Jacob in the desert, when he put a few way-side stones together as a pillow for his weary head. That rude masonry was the foundation of a shining stair on which angels trod in ministries to man.

There were towers, palaces, and kingly courts erected in the primal days of old, and cities and capitols of magnificence appeared wherever man extended his domain. But, of all ages and lands, no grander achievement has masonry ever accomplished than that of building Solomon's temple. It was erected in a time of peace, when the Lord had put Israel's enemies "under the sole of his feet." Hiram, the king of Tyre, proffered the aid of his subjects, and access to distant forests and quarries, and the stupendous undertaking was begun. The fraternity between Solomon and Hiram extended to the servants of both; and on mountain and in mine there was harmony wherever the laborers wrought. One great will seemed to control the many thousand workmen, all duly and well qualified for their respective stations. The hands of wood-hewers and stone-squarers moved as the one strong right hand of Solomon the Wise. So completely did the workmen understand the plan, and supplement each other's labors, that there was neither hammer, nor axe, nor any tool of iron heard in the temple while it was rising, from its foundation to its dome. There was such accuracy of calculation, such exact preparation and adjustment of parts, such strict adherence to the original design, that, although at such distances measured, shaped and pointed, the stones and beams of the immense structure were fixed in their places and ranged into general symmetry almost as noiselessly as the petals and stamens of a lily that opens into bloom in a summer morning. The unity was so complete that never a jar nor jostle disturbed the process of the builders.

There is something in such precalculated order and patient industry as this—the masonry of plan and labor—that symbolizes the operations of the church of Christ. There is a distinct and comprehensive work, inspired by the divine will, ever going on in the human soul, shaping itself in consecrated life among people of every name and nation, the wide world over. The quiet, but sure and steady rising of Solomon's temple beautifully illustrates the rising of the spiritual temple—the dwelling-place of the Most High—upon the earth. There is a charm of variety in unity, of peace in busy toil, of fraternity in separate spheres, homes, and occupations. God permits such blessed fellowship of love and reciprocity of confidence in chosen circles here below. As in the building of the temple there was a masonry of mechanics, and as in social life there is a masonry of kindred minds, so in the universal church of Christ, there is a masonry of sympathetic souls. "All things work together for good to them that love God." And love to God implies love to man.

The foundation of a building is its groundwork, its rest, and its support. Take away the foundation of the building where we worship or dwell, and all its other portions would fall to ruins in a moment. Yet the essential part on which the superstructure stands is hidden. We see the steps, the walls, the ceiling; but the most important part is not intended to be seen. That, in a building, which is for strength and support, is never essentially visible.

So the Rock of Ages on which the Christian church is built, although concealed from mortal sight, is its sure and eternal base. This is why the church has not fallen — why it can not fall; this is why it has stood, and shall forever stand, the combined attacks of all enemies; this is why the gates of hell shall not prevail against it. It is founded on a Rock. Take away from the Christian system the infinite Christ, and the whole fabric must fall. Where the divinity of Christ is denied, the church totters, scatters, admits the frost and snow to its altars, and becomes a fallen mass of ruins. The winds of false doctrine howl its requiem. But the true foundation-stone, the Christ of God, the Jesus of the people, is tried. The eternal One came down to our depths of misery and want, down to the deepest stratum of humanity, suffered, died the victim of malignant hate, and all for love! He seemed forsaken of the Father. But he bore the awful test of tears and blood. He was tried. As pressure brings out the fragrance of flowers — as night brings out the beauty of the stars — so did Christ's suffering reveal his love.

But the foundation has been tried by skeptics and critics in all ages of the Christian era. From Celsus to Renan, Jesus has stood the attacks of hostile enemies. Some crafty scholars have tried to argue him away as a myth — an ideal; but he has a history of solid facts. His record is ineffaceable. It has left tallying testimony in the world's annals, and in the rocks, in the circling suns, and in the consciences of men. Christ has stood well the blows of every sledge of infidelity; and he is to-day, in person and in character, real to more thoughtful souls than in any period of the past. Criticism has only proved the tried stone to be precious. The commanding edifice of his truth has been rising and shining in silent increase, in spaciousness and in beauty, as the wonderful temple rose before the busy builders' hands at Jerusalem in noiseless but positive accession every day.

The church of Christ consists of all true believers of every land, age, complexion, and tribe. This structure is bounded by no narrow ecclesiastical limits. It is greater than any titled organization. It can not be fully represented by theological views; nor can its census be taken from denominational statistics. No sect can justly claim, however correct its orthodoxy or high its standard of spiritual proprieties, to be the only church of Christ. The New Testament knows of no exclusive community organized as the alone visible church. No society of kindred believers can arrogate to itself the ministry, the means of grace, and the sacraments. The foundation is Christ, the apostles, and the prophets: Jesus Christ being the chief, the corner-stone, binding the old and the new dispensations into one. The church of God is the purchase of his blood — not a company united under a human head or by a human bond. The base and boundary of all believers are broad as the Bible, the Christ, the apostles and the prophets. The Lamb's Book of Life is the only correct register of believers. The Church of the First Born is not Roman nor Protestant, Greek nor Anglican, Episcopal nor Presbyterian, Baptist nor Methodist, although it includes members in all these branches. It is no national church, for no nation under heaven is big enough to give it name. It is nothing less nor lower than the great multitude which no man can number, of all kindreds and peoples and tongues. The foundation laid in Zion is immensely broad — broader than Plymouth Rock — broader than all the Augsburgs in Germany — broader than the seven hills by the Tiber. The corner-stone in Zion is firm enough for an immortal superstructure that shall rise above the sun.

"One family we dwell in him:
One church above, beneath,

Though now divided by the stream —
  The narrow stream of death.
One army of the living God,
  To his command we bow;
Part of the host have crossed the flood,
  And part are crossing now."

Man, the lord of creation, needs shelter more than any other creature that breathes. He is the most defenceless of beings. Without a dwelling-place he would be the shortest-lived of animals. Without a home, the forces of nature which he now controls and makes minister to his comfort, would be his speedy destroyers. This want of shelter conditions all other relations in life. It creates the family, fixes a place of habitation, institutes order, government, security and strength. Humanity must have a home. The house is to the family what the body is to the soul, an indispensable tabernacle.

The Christian church is the believers' house for refuge, culture, and repose. As men can not live upon the earth and be men without a house of some description, neither can Christians, as such, live anywhere without some kind of association and communion. There exists a necessity for an organized and visible church. There must be law with love, assimilation, fraternity, mutual support and defence. There is a sacred affinity of hearts which the gospel recognizes and promotes. The members of the same family eat from the same table. So all true Christians have common access to the heavenly supplies. Tear down the house and you dissolve the family, and society would be in ruins. Tear down the church, and Christianity would perish. A man can not live a separated life. The laws of his being imply association and obligation to certain rules and regulations, pre-arranged for every one born into the race. Nor can a Christian live a separated life. No disciple can thrive as an absolute ecclesiastical independent. There is here and there an enthusiasm which ignores church organization altogether, contemns all formularies, rejects the ministry, and asks that men be let alone with their Bibles, to worship in unembarrassed isolation. Suppose that a house leaks in water through the roof, or lets in wind through a crevice in the wall, or has some defective timbers, shall the family, imperfectly sheltered, destroy the structure entirely, and take to the outer rain, the cold, and the storm, each member for himself? Suppose that because the church is deficient in some part of its superstructure, admits a little frost at times, has a shelving cornice, a crooked post, a knotty plank, shall Christians batter it down and disperse, shelterless, single, and alone, to contend with such a frowning world as this? With such human nature as ours built in, could perfection be expected? If the church were disorganized, what confusion, sorrow, and loss! No, we are members one of another, compacted and built on one foundation. Religious life depends more on the church than some persons seem willing to admit. Fellowship overcomes many a difficulty, quickens many a conviction, expands many a charity, and saves many a soul. Christ has established a church — a building — a visible structure — and is himself the corner-stone. The disciples of him who had not where to lay his head shall never be unhoused. And this house, founded on a

Rock, rises every day a little nearer heaven. Its design is after the model of our Father's house with many mansions. Our Babels do not help us up to God. Our views, our schools, our opinions, our theologies are only chaff. The true church is built of living stones. Our schemes result in confusion and disaster when the storm comes, and the flood. The Master Builder alone could lay the foundation-stone of the temple, and this he did in Zion when he gave himself to die. God builds immortalities upon this foundation. He takes many a rough stone from nature's quarry, and, by the sharp edges of discipline, shapes it for position on the Rock, Christ Jesus. Soul by soul, man by man, the world is brought to Christ, fixed, stablished, settled on him. Men may amuse, entertain, instruct, excite, astonish; but no one can build save God alone. All the materials that masons may quarry, square, polish and seal upon a false foundation will soon crush and crumble to the dust. The wise builder knows upon what his workmanship shall rest. Its symmetry, its compactness, its fidelity of joint, its utility, everything depends upon the corner-stone. So, exactly, in the church. A society built upon any man, even upon an apostle, *as* an apostle, will, in the pressure of ages, swerve and fall, however vast the pile; and the greater its dimensions, the more appalling its overthrow at last. The true church does not rest on Peter, or Paul, or Luther, or Calvin, or Wesley, but only, squarely and forever, on Jesus Christ: He is the tried and precious corner-stone on which all believers build their lives, of every age, nation, circumstance and name.

The foundation is a *stone,* true and precious. The word indicates stability and strength. Stone is the solidest of earth's building materials. Rock is the deep, underlying support of the soil, with its forest, meadow, and mansion. It seems strange that any thoughtful mind should ever look upon Peter, a mortal, a fallible man, a man of mistakes, cowardice and impulse, except only when held by the power of his Lord, as the rock-foundation of the church. When, on one occasion, our Saviour questioned his disciples on their knowledge of his own personality and work, Peter answered, "Thou art *the Christ*, the Son of the living God." And Jesus said, "*Thou* art Peter; and upon *this* rock will I build my church." That is to say, On this rock *which thou hast confessed by heavenly inspiration* — upon *myself*, the Son of the living God, as thou hast said — upon *this* will I build my church. Now, has the church, since the days of the apostles, been resting upon Christ or upon men? Some of Peter's successors, according to the Roman calendar, have been of doubtful integrity, some of feeble spiritual pulse, and of influence none the purest. The present Pope Pius was not quite sure whether he was infallible, and to be certain, let fallible men decide! Has the holy truth of God been built on sand or on granite — on human characters, changeful as the clouds, or on Christ, "the same yesterday, and to-day, and forever?" Oh, not on dying men, not on broken arches of humanity, but on the precious, permanent corner-stone once laid in Zion, rests the church to-day! The Rock of Ages is tried and true.

"The tempest rages through the earth around,
Tossing the ocean into mountain waves;
Thrones shake and totter as the storm-wind raves,
And mightiest empires tremble at the sound;
What is there stable 'mid this wild uproar?
The church heeds not the angry billows' shock;
Thy church, O Lord, is founded on a Rock!"

On the stormy southwestern coast of England is a massive column of masonry, resting upon a desolate island rock, a league or two from shore. It lifts its brilliant light steadily as a star along the firmament, to warn the mariner of breakers, and of the yawning gulfs below. It is the renowned Eddystone light-house. A hundred years ago, the architect who proposed to erect in such a dreary place a light-house — a column of stone strong enough to defy the howling blasts and surging tides of the sea — was laughed to scorn. The proposition was treated as the dream of an enthusiast. The people said that no edifice could possibly be reared in such a place to stand against the sweep of storm and billow. Yet the builder, just *because* of the great danger, was the more determined to succeed. Almost alone, he began his work. He cleared a level on the isolated rock for a foundation. The corner-stone was tried and laid. Layer after layer of adamant went down in solid strata, the structure rising into view only to excite the ridicule of spectators on the shore. They smiled contemptuously, and said the first fierce storm would sweep the masonry away. The storms came, one after another, and, like broadsides from a battery, drove the workmen from their places on the walls. But as the winds abated, the work went on. Tempests were but arguments for perfect work. The howling sea, by its very madness, said, "Build strong. Bind the walls." Stone by stone the column rose as a monument of patience and perseverance, toward the clouds. At length, after years of labor, the cap-stone was laid, and soon the cheery beacon-light from Eddystone danced triumphantly over the billows.

Even then, opinionated prophets would say, "Never mind. Only wait. It will fail yet. It can not stand against the great storms, such as we *have* seen. It will yet give way before the tides." In three years one of the great storms did come. The people on shore shuddered for the fate of the keepers of Eddystone light-house. It was a night of awful crash and thunderbolt and roar along the coast. In the morning after the tempest hundreds of people hastened to look toward the sea, lest the beautiful column should be missing. Anxious eyes, through telescopes, turned hopefully and yet fearfully to the ominous southwest. The universal question of the hour was only, "Has that majestic structure been swallowed in the waves?" But how great was the joy of its friends, how bitter the disappointment of its enemies, how intense the astonishment of all, when, through the misty atmosphere of morning, the magnificent, upright proportions of Eddystone light-house were seen, still bearing its turrets to the sky, still throwing its radiance along the restless sea! Not a stone was displaced. Not a ray of light was extinguished. The foundation stood the test for itself, and for all the superstructure which it bore. It still stands. The tornadoes of a hundred years have assaulted it in vain. It rests on a tried stone—a sure foundation, a "well-formed, true and trusty" corner-stone.

So stands the church of Jesus Christ to-day. Established in a time of peace, its corner-stone bound together Jews and Gentiles into one broad foundation-square for an enduring edifice. As a light-house built to warn and save men, it was laughed to scorn at first. The tempests of persecution well nigh swept the builders from their work. But they had courageous hearts and brawny arms; they rallied against opposition, built the stronger, pressed forward, initiated new builders according to the simple ritual of the gospel, extended the walls, and toiled away by faith before the powers of pagan, infidel, skeptic and philosopher. And still the glorious structure rises toward the skies. Its cap-stone shall glitter forever with the reflected radiance from the very throne of God. Eighteen centuries have not accumulated storms enough to disturb the "well-formed, tried and trusty" corner-stone. Silently as the temple on Moriah, savingly as the Eddystone tower of adamant, the church of Christ rises with life and light for all the world.

"On the Rock of Ages founded,
What can shake her sure repose?
With salvation's walls surrounded,
She can smile at all her foes."

If the church were built on anything less true and precious than the Son of God, the storms of persecution would have leveled its walls to the dust of oblivion long years ago. But the foundation is eternal and immutable Truth, and the blood of the martyrs is the cement that sealed the granite facts of all history into the masonry of this spiritual edifice. It is impregnable and must stand forever. All its materials are prepared with the gauge and gavel of truth; every wall is raised to the plumb-line of rectitude; each duty is squared by the compass of virtue; the whole structure is cemented by brotherly love. It is a temple of living stones—a temple of imperishable thoughts and deeds, shaped and inlaid to the will of Him who built the universe; and it is evermore illuminated by the Holy Spirit.

Christian men and women, if only we could draw aside the veil that conceals the shining ones in glory, and send up the question,

"What is the foundation on which you built while strangers in this wilderness?" they would answer, as with a bugle shout, "Jesus — Jesus only!" Glorified St. Paul would repeat from the celestial heights what he preached on earth, "There is no other name given under heaven or among men whereby they can be saved." And all the redeemed would answer in full chorus, Behold the foundation laid in Zion, the tried and precious corner-stone." Jesus — Jesus only, Jesus forever! The loudest hallelujahs are in honor of his name.

Sinner, troubled, tempted, downcast, undone — come, build your life anew in Jesus. Bring your burdened heart — your restless self — your all, and learn the secret of real living in the blessed will of God. Millions, as wretched and miserable as the vilest outcast who now breathes the air in infamy, have come, trusted their all upon this sure foundation, and are smiling and waving palms in heaven. Come, that you may be ready to exult in victory over death, and say, "I know in whom I have believed." You will need a rest and a refuge *then*. How soon the *then* of death is here!

The darkness gathers. The storm mutters. The lightning flashes. Heart and flesh shall fail. You will soon be overtaken and overcome. Accept the Saviour *now.* The invitation is unqualified, unlimited, universal.

> "Lift up th' eternal gates,
> The doors wide open fling;
> Enter, ye nations that obey
> The statutes of your King!"

THE BRICKLAYER.

"Ye shall no more give the people straw to make brick as heretofore: let them go and gather straw for themselves.

"Let there more work be laid upon the men, that they may labor therein: and let them not regard vain words." — EXODUS V. 7, 9.

CHAPTER III.

THE BRICKLAYER.

THE first account of brick-making in the Bible is in the book of Genesis, where record is made of Noah's descendants journeying from the east and settling on the plains of Shinar.

The tents of the moving masses had hitherto been their most substantial dwellings; but now there is to be marked an era of change in the material of their habitations. The transient and flimsy fabric of pole and canvas is to give place to buildings with fixed foundations. Wandering tribes are about to assume permanent abodes, and to establish citizenship and civil relations.

The family now recognizes the community; society takes its place in the economy of Providence. The land of Shinar, on the rich plains

6

that bordered the Euphrates, was beautiful and luxurious, but destitute of stone; and its soil yielded no lime for cement, and hence, in the early history of architecture, there arose a necessity for invention. The sandy clay was found to be easily moulded and sun-burnt into convenient forms that would answer in the place of stones; and a kind of bitumen or slime which floated on the ponds and marshes, was substituted for mortar to bind the bricks into solid walls.

It was here, of such materials, and by men theretofore of one language, that the tower of Babel was attempted, as a refuge against another flood. The people were not willing to trust God's word, though stamped with the rainbow seal, that there should be no more deluge, but rather inclined to believe in brick of their own hands' making than in the promise of the Almighty.

Cities and towers from this time forward began to dot the post-diluvian world. The manufacture and laying of bricks were the occupations of multitudes of busy men. There are still in existence in Egypt both public and private buildings erected with the kind of materials described by Moses in the Pentateuch. The Babylonian bricks were about one foot square, and three and a half inches thick. They bore various inscriptions and patterns on their surface, cast in their moulding. Really the art of printing might be said to date its origin in this custom. Old bricks have been discovered at Nineveh and Thebes bearing the ovals of a king, and the names and offices of the priests.

Both sun-dried and kiln-burnt bricks were common in the treasure cities and granaries of lower Egypt. The clay from the banks of the Nile was carried in baskets, thrown into mass, saturated, and trodden into the proper temper by the feet of the workmen. It was a most fatiguing and perilous toil. Nahum refers to the severity of such service in his prophecy, iii. 14, "Draw thee waters for the siege, fortify thy strongholds: go into clay, and tread the mortar, make strong the brick-kiln."

Wherever there was any difficulty in procuring desirable building stones, the Romans, in later ages, resorted to the use of bricks.

The Roman bricks were from eighteen to thirty inches in length, nine inches in width, and two and three-fifths inches in thickness, and originated a style of architecture peculiar to their shape. Bricks were less used during the early part of the middle ages; but about the twelfth century were generally employed in Northern Italy, and in the adjacent provinces. By the sixteenth century, brick almost superseded stone, and many of the great cathedrals and prominent public works of engineering were executed of bricks even where stone was accessible. In later years the taste is changing again, and stone-work comes to the front in fashionable architecture, and bricks are pressed into rear walls and unpretending structures.

The various colored bricks, red, yellow, blue and brown are obtained from clays of peculiar tints. The Philadelphia pressed bricks have a brilliant red appearance, while the common and scarcely less beautiful bricks of Milwaukee are cream-tinged, and in those cities the walls hold their primitive colors; while in Pittsburgh, Wheeling, and other places, whatever may have been the original hue of houses, they soon become shadowed with the smoke and soot of the bituminous fires. And so does many a man's religion, however bright and clear at first, sometimes become tinged with the prevailing atmospheres. It were well, however, if the shade on men gets no thicker than on houses.

There are solid bricks, red and clean at heart, in the walls of the dimmest old church under the settling smoke. So be it evermore, beyond our sight, with the varied human portions that compose the temple of the living God, though oft obscured without and dull with the dust and grime of business — may they be pure and clean within!

A large and profitable commerce is carried on along the upper Ohio River shores, in the manufacture of fire-bricks — a tile for furnaces and hearths, prepared of superior material for which the West Virginia hills are famous, and burnt in a porcelain kiln of manifold severer heat than that of ordinary fires, and free in their composition from lime, magnesia, and iron, and matured in their elements to avoid unequal contraction and expansion by any temperature to which they may be subsequently exposed. These fire-bricks are costly and rare in comparison with the great bulk of bricks that go into the world's material structures. But they are indispensable for certain places. They do not warp nor crumble at the force of the flame — they are true to their shape and weight in the time of trial.

And there are fire-brick men in the Christian church. They come of royal humble blood. They are found in obscure families. They are searched out by Providences, tried in the furnaces of affliction and fused into condensed power by peculiar agencies, for setting in prominent places in the great spiritual temple. Like the three Hebrew children, they stand the fire. Men who have passed through intense sorrow and suffering are the truest for health and for altar tests. Men who have been disciplined by loss, by ridicule, by persecution, are the men to set in exposed places where ordinary human nature would yield and give way.

Luther, Calvin, Knox, Wesley, Campbell, Stockton — these were fire-brick men when the Bible was assailed by the hot blasts of infidelity — rare, firm, invincible — and they filled their places well. The church always needs such men, and always puts them in their proper stations.

Brick-making in its varied forms, as an art, is, we see, one of the oldest and most important. It has prominence among the Bible occupations, monuments itself in architecture, and has honorable mention in history from the days of the Babylonian captivity, when poor men toiled in sand and sun as slaves, until the present day, when freedmen with their own hands rear colleges for themselves and children, and all ancient and modern Pharaohs, with their horses and chariots, hounds, marshals, and all, are swallowed together in the sea!

Asiatic architecture, among the Chaldees, produced the brick type, and was the first to introduce the arch as a distinct element of construction. This is considered to be the most difficult part of the art. The cutting of bricks to a separate bend or angle, and gauging the circle for strength and beauty, is one of the intricate tasks of the bricklayer. The pier and arch compose a distinct system, while the post and lintel are subjective in their origin to a symbolized religion. By these forms, variously wrought and ornamented, special deities and hero gods were personated. By this means the earliest poetry of paganism was embodied. And to this day the temples of idolatry are more for the accommodation of the eye than the ear; more for sight-seeing than for hearing instruction.

In architecture there can be traced, as on a winding stair, an advancement from crudity to magnificence; and this fact symbolizes the building of man's moral character, as he rises from the dreams and transiency of childhood into the symmetrical solidity of maturer years.

A particular building may be finished, may become old, may be pointed out as a ruin; but architecture is the soul of building; *it* continues from age to age, always approaching perfection, coming up toward the model of "the house not made with hands, eternal in the heavens." So mind is never stationary, although the body may cease to grow — may begin to crumble down. The soul, immortal, and aspiring, forever ascends the mystic winding stair, each step leading to some new range of mental illumination, and to the apprehension of some undiscovered truth nearer and nearer to God.

Man rises from the flower-garden of infancy, where a blooming acre is a world, and a loving mother is immaculate, to the presence of the Eternal, to roam at will his universe of suns; for vision and knowledge shall increase with the capacities of the ever-enlarging soul.

But there rises a train of thoughts from the subject which may be profitable in its closer analogies and suggestions.

The children of Israel are in cruel bondage to Pharaoh. They are obliged to make brick for his cities, treasure-vaults, and palaces. Although their toil is arduous and unpaid, they are humble, patient, and uncomplaining. Hard work is the only school where persons honorably graduate in lessons of modesty. Lowly vocations insure good manners.

The hard-worked Hebrews merely ask for a brief vacation from labor — a three days' journey to make sacrifice to God, as idolaters were permitted to do to their gods. The incessant brick-making would cease but for a short half-week, and then the people, refreshed and re-united, would resume their labor, and more than recover their borrowed time.

Pharaoh has already had many cities and towers erected by these captives' hands, and it is reasonable to hope for a little holiday that should be a holy day indeed. But the tyrant barbarously denies the request, and adds insult to injury by calling them idlers and their worship vanity. The same day the Israelites requested the favor to worship God, Pharaoh commanded harder tasks than ever: "Ye shall no more give the people straw to make brick, as heretofore. Let them go and gather straw for themselves. Let there more work be laid upon the men, that they may labor therein; and let them not regard vain words."

What the use of straw was in making bricks is not exactly clear. It is conjectured by some that it was to heat the kilns, by others that it was a sort of covering to prevent the fresh-moulded bricks from cracking under the violent heating of the sun. This opinion is strengthened by the record in Vitruvius, who says that the best bricks were made in the spring or autumn, that they might dry in an equal heat, the midsummer solstice being so intense as to form a crust upon the bricks, while they would remain moist and soft within. Still another opinion, and perhaps the correct one, is that the straw was wrought into the compact body of the bricks, owing to the alluvial nature of the Nile deposits, from which they were made. At any rate, the straw was a necessity, and Pharaoh not only acts the tyrant, but the fool, in shutting off the supply. It was to his own interest to furnish straw; but the common sense of the monarch is overbalanced by his passion. And *he* is the man who presumes to call God's words vain words. He shall learn better when the Red-Sea billows chill his royal blood and close over his crownéd brow.

The haughty Egyptian ruler who insists upon the usual tale of bricks, on time to the minute, and made to the standard, may early learn the proverb, "A drowning man catches at a straw." He may yet have a want, and not a means of supply! But while the power is yet in his hand he drives for more work, harder work, and withholds the material. This was the answer to the desire of the people to make sacrifices to God.

Nothing for the Lord; all for Pharaoh. The order was enforced. The people scattered over the land to gather stubble for straw. The taskmasters hurried them up, whipped them to their work, demanding the full daily task to be done, and well done, to the last inch, and to the very moment.

Such is slavery. It has no mercy. It lashes as chatteled herds, immortal souls. Darker and drearier grew the night. But "man's extremity was God's opportunity." The harder a ball is thrown down the higher it rebounds. Sometimes the worse the better. "Who is the Lord?" says Pharaoh. *He has learned who he is.*

The devil has his Egypt, and his work to be done, his castles to build, his palaces of revelry to keep going, his theaters to run, his saloons to be sustained. He has enterprises on his hands immense as pyramids, and he uses men. He has millions of captives in his hands, moulding his mud, baking his brick, and enlarging his possessions. And he tyrannizes over his subjects in cruelest exaction. He is the Shylock greedy for his pound of flesh; and he takes it at whatever smart. He does cut after men's flesh! Sinners are the bondmen, making brick for Satan without pay and without straw, paying over blood, bone, and spirit for the horrible opportunity — abject, hated, hurried, starving, dying slaves, doing their haughty master's bidding.

You read of old Pharaoh of Egypt, and your blood tingles at his heartless dealings with the Hebrews; your soul leaps up and shouts at the joy of hating such a tyrant; and you can hardly choke down your hallelujahs at *his* choking in the sea! But how is it, this hour, with your own allegiance? Whom do you serve? Are you serving God in newness of life — in Canaanward liberty marching on — or are you drudging in the sand, scraping after stubble, and sweltering under the fierce suns of Satan's slavery? Either you are bond, or you are free.

There is a man who gives his time and talent to hoarding money, to broadening his estates, to office-hunting, to fashion, politics, and pleasure, and becomes so absorbed in mammon that he can not lift a thought to heaven; so engaged with self that he feels no concern for others. That man is a bondman and a brickmaker for the cruel old Pharaoh, who still presses the people into his service—brickmaking for the devil is he, without straw, with his face to the sand, and his back to the sun.

The word "bond" is applied to the mode of laying bricks side by side, and one upon another, with a view to secure the greatest amount of strength with given space and material, and to produce a symmetrical appearance. There are several kinds of bond in the art, but in each the same precaution is required in distributing the cement, and so fixing the bricks that the joints shall never be immediately over one another. The workman's phrase is that bricks must "break bond." But to break bond in bricklaying is just the reverse of breaking bond anywhere else. Here it means to hold fast.

A man, building character, must break bond as a bricklayer. His thoughts, purposes, and actions must interlap and interlock, cross over each other, and be sealed by brotherly love. He must build in much for strength and little for show. Comparatively few bricks go into the street-side wall of a house. The materials that compose the rear walls, gables, and cross partitions must be as firmly burnt and carefully laid in as the stenciled rows that face the thoroughfares. So a man must make himself strong, not merely in a single trait, or truth, but build his character through and through by plumb and level.

He must square himself up heavenward by well-adjusted proportions of reading, business, meditation, and religion. His works must measure up even against his words. He must provide windows of illumination and doors for his guests. Some men are built like jails. They are blind walls and gloom all the way up; their eyes are cross-barred with forbidding frowns. If there are emotions within they are prisoners. Not a solitary tear can escape the sentinels.

Now, if in the ideal of the apostle Paul, a man's body is a house, let it be a home and not a prison for the soul. How beautiful the house that stands square and level against the storms, that has ample windows, welcoming doors, airy and cheery parlors, music, conversation, books, bounty, fragrance, congenial company, for dweller and visitor and guest! As a pleasant residence goes into form with every item of material accurately calculated, set and sealed into its place, so does a man build himself into symmetrical character. It is no chance-work. The more exact every thought, the more refined every impulse, the more polished every sentiment, the stronger and safer his manhood, and the more room for radiance through the windows of his soul. Many a young man is building his own penitentiary out of the materials God has put within his reach for a comely and consecrated home. People, people, let us build choicefully, build diligently, build into our life-dwelling the best materials, make windows, break the bonds! To the rhythm and cheer of the poet's* song, let us busily build:

"For the structure that we raise
 Time is with materials filled;
Our to-days and yesterdays
 Are the blocks with which we build.

"Truly shape and fashion these;
 Leave no yawning gaps between;
Think not, because no man sees
 Such things will remain unseen.

"Let us do our work as well,
 Both the unseen and the seen;
Make the house where God may dwell,
 Beautiful, entire, and clean.

"Else our lives are incomplete,
 Standing in these walls of Time,
Broken stairways, where the feet
 Stumble as they seek to climb.

"Build to-day, then, strong and sure,
 With a firm and ample base;
And ascending and secure
 Shall to-morrow find its place."

* Longfellow.

The bricklayer accomplishes his work little by little. Brick by brick the greatest cathedral rises. One brick appears but a trifle; but such trifles aggregated make temples and mighty cities. This is God's way in nature. "First the seed, then the blade, then the ear, then the full corn in the ear." So human character is developed. Twenty-one years of patience and culture are required to put a ballot in a baby's hand. Faith is not so much a climax as an expanding agent. It may be increased in any heart. "O Lord, increase our faith!"

In the far South Seas are many broad islands, with lofty mountains and luxuriant plains. Tall trees stand laden with delicious fruits in the groves. Rare birds warble in the forests. Crystal streams gurgle from the hills, ripple and dance through the woodlands, and, swelling into rivers along the wide valleys, push vast currents of fresh water out into the bitter sea. New-made worlds are these islands, and homes of multitudes of people. But the materials of which they are built have been collected from ten thousand marble quarries in the deep, selected atom by atom, shaped, fixed, and sealed together with the exactest care and skill. Islands now, but once they were infinitesimal particles floating in the salt sea waves. The mechanics that dived after the materials and brought them to their places were tiny insects smaller than the head of a pin. From lime in the water-drops these little masons and bricklayers put down the foundation and reared the superstructure of continents in the agitated seas. What a craft of architects are they, uniformed in regalia of crystal, busy for evermore in building happy homes for men! "Here a little, and there a little," and the stupendous work is done.

Thus, Christian, do you build your character. You may be unseen and unknown, but you are progressing as long as you believe and keep busy. Your very tears and sighs go into substantial structure beneath your pilgrim feet. A more than coral continent is shaping as the homeland of your soul. Be patient. Persevere. Build away in dark or light. God helps you every hour. Though you blunder with your A B C's, though you be worried with the primer of your discipleship, though you can not begin to read divine providences now, *master the alphabet*, and you have the key-words to unlock a blessed immortality. The words of sacrifice are not vain words. Press forward, and the monotonies of service will modulate, sweeten, and ring out into the archangelic song of victory over death, and welcome to your house "not made with hands, eternal in the heavens!"

"Low on the ground an acorn lies;
Little by little it mounts to the skies;
Shadow and shelter for wandering herds—
Home for a hundred singing birds.
Little by little the great rock grew,
Long, long ago, when the world was new;
Slowly and silently, stately and free,
Cities of coral under the sea
Little by little are builded—while so
The ages come and the ages go.

"Little by little all things are done;
So are the crowns of the faithful won;
So is heaven in our hearts begun,
With work and weeping and laughter and play;

Little by little the longest day,
And the longest life are passing away—
Passing without return—while so
Our spring-time comes, and our winters go."

From the abundant materials which God has placed within our reach, let us build ourselves up into eternity. Upon the Rock of Ages let us build. A thought, a word, an act, hopes, tears, and joys—all these on Christ we build, breaking bonds, little by little, all the time. By breaths, songs, charities, prayers, deeds, let us build up character into the very heavens!

THE FOUNDER.

"As they gather silver, and brass, and iron, and lead, and tin, into the midst of the furnace, to blow the fire upon it, to melt it: so will I gather you in mine anger and in my fury, and I will leave you there and melt you."—EZEKIEL xxii. 20.

CHAPTER IV.

THE FOUNDER.

THE furnace figure of Ezekiel is a striking example of divine instruction adopting the phraseology of worldly work. The secular is seized upon to illustrate the spiritual. It is the common method of the Scriptures to explain the unseen by the seen; things remote by things at hand; the heavenly messages and meanings by current forms and movements. The Bible is a book of object-lessons for the eye, the ear, the imagination. The poetry of inspiration is radiant with vivid pictures. They glitter in unfading beauty from Genesis to Revelation. They are very old and very new. The prophecies, especially, glow with portraitures of things sublime, familiar, and significant. The imagery of Ezekiel is of matchless range and exhaustless beauty.

The process of founding or moulding metals into form is implied in the language of the prophet. He was not so wrapt in celestial theories as to be indifferent to earthly sights and sounds. The religion he represented did not express itself in abstract monotonies. God used Ezekiel as a man acquainted with common things, mingling with common people; and not as an airy stranger, half let down to earth and half gone up to heaven — talking in a foreign tongue and a lofty tone, distantly, indistinctly, professionally, as a mysterious being — less than an angel, and yet more than a man. He talked about furnaces and metals. He drew analogies from ordinary occupations; and under inspiration he moulded many model thoughts and themes for the minor and plainer prophets of all subsequent ages.

It is the business of the founder to take advantage of a common law — that by which water seeks its level, conforming to the shape of the vessel into which it pours. It first finds the bottom, then spreads, rises, touches outmost verges, until every accessible vacuum is reached. The bulk of water is then a perfect model of the interior of the vessel. Let it freeze, and the solid body of ice be extracted, and every feature of the mould, faults and all, is accurately preserved. So is it the business of the Christian teacher to take advantage of the common law of resemblances and analogies, and to illustrate truth and duty by pictures from every-day observation. The prophets so instructed the people, and were understood; and the apostles followed their example — an example made emphatic by the methods of Christ himself — and were never accused of secularizing holy things, except by the Pharisees, who were too religious to allow a few heads of wheat to be rubbed out of its chaff by hungry men on the Sabbath, and yet not too religious to bruise people to death with stones for entertaining opinions at variance with their own, any day and anywhere.

Founding embraces all the operations of reducing ores and smelting and casting metals, from coin to cannon, from printing-types to cylinders and bells. The art is one of the most ancient. Tubal Cain was skilled in working metals. It is evident that copper was, if not the only metal known for a long period, the most abundant. It was universally used for ornaments, utensils, and arms. Iron was of later discovery. But the very earliest nations successfully wrought in copper, brass, and gold. It is said that the Egyptians had the art of tempering brass, and giving it sharp and lasting edge in articles of cutlery. This statement is corroborated by the fact that wherever the word "steel" occurs in our version of the Bible, the original is *brass*. What we know as steel is called "northern iron" by Jeremiah. One of the first references to the subject in the writings of Moses is where Abraham's servant gave Rebecca a golden ear-ring of half a shekel weight, and two bracelets for her hands of ten shekels weight of gold. In making the presentation to the beautiful and courteous damsel at the well, he referred to his master's riches, especially mentioning silver and gold. The various passages in the Old Testament touching this subject prove an extensive employment in metals in the times of Jacob and Joseph; and the fact that they were used for luxury and ornament argues that considerable progress had been attained in the art. The ancient sculptors were workers in metal. Bezaleel, of the tribe of Judah, a shrewd and skillful genius in his day, devised elaborate works of gold, silver, and brass. He, Aholiab, of the tribe of Dan, and others of similar tastes and training, were the artists who executed the ornate work of the Tabernacle.

Among the Egyptians the use of metal dates from the earliest historical records. In the excavations at Nineveh, various bronze ornaments, which had evidently been cast in a mould, were found; and several specimens of these curiosities may to-day be seen in the British Museum. The Israelites cast a molten calf as a god, while Moses communed with the Lord on the mount. The artificer engaged by Solomon to decorate the temple, a thousand years before the birth of Christ, was Hiram, a native of Tyre, "cunning to work all works of brass." History testifies that some of these productions were cast, and that some were wrought.

In the time of Homer, there were arms,

statues, and ornaments made in Greece. The first and most simple process seems to have been hammer-work. Lumps of the material were beaten into the required form; and if the work projected were too large to be forged of one piece, several were shaped, and all fitted and fastened together by keys. Herodotus distinguishes between the hammer-wrought metals and those that were cast. In the time of Moses, the lawgiver commanded that the brazen censers should be beaten out into plates for covering the Tabernacle.

It is difficult to determine when the art of casting metal in moulds was first employed. Its progress was gradual. Simple as the process appears to us, it has been developed by successive inventions. At first the metal was melted into a mass, and then beaten out into proposed shapes. The next step in discovery was to melt and mould the material into form, leaving the statue solid. The third method or step in discovery was to cast in a mould, with a center-piece or core, by which to limit the thickness of the metal. The last of these distinct stages was known at a period some five hundred years before the Christian era; and there has been no radical improvement in the art since that time.

The ancient Romans were inferior to the Greeks in works of art. Zenodorus, however, imitating the productions of Greece, executed some splendid designs in the time of Nero, among which was a colossal statue of the emperor, one hundred and ten feet high. But Pliny, who lived in the reign of Vespasian, records the decline of the art, and a sad lack of skill and ambition among the artists of his time. Furnaces of considerable size were built in the days of Queen Elizabeth; and until the seventeenth century the metals of Britain were smelted by wood fuel, but the demand becoming so great, the forests were exhausted. It was only after many patient experiments that coal was brought into use. The increase of civilization augmenting the commerce, the manufacture of iron in its various forms has at length become an immense business, not only in Great Britian, but also in the United States. Pittsburgh is known the world over as the "Iron City." About two-sevenths of all the iron consumed in this country is manufactured here. There are upward of thirty large iron-mills, working up, on an average, some twelve hundred tons of metal every day. Besides these, there are eight steel and two copper-mills of first-class capacity, employed both day and night. The work turned out from these establishments goes into a thousand uses in as many different localities, near and far, substantial testimonials of the genius and industry of this city. There is a single mill in this vicinity that turns out more iron than all the mills of England a hundred years ago.

These mills and foundries furnish direct employment to some fifteen thousand men, besides business of a kindred nature to more than twice as many more. These people are our neighbors and fellow-citizens, an honor to the State, and eminently deserving of Christian sympathies and acquaintance. There should be a better understanding between the churches and the mills. There are vacant pews enough in Pittsburgh to accommodate thousands of these workingmen, who may never have been visited in all the years of their toil, and personally invited to a seat, and assured a welcome in the sanctuary. As Protestants, we are sadly slower in this legitimate work than our industrious and devoted neighbors — the Roman Catholics. We may learn the very first lessons of evangelization from those whom we are wont to criticise and avoid. There is no cathedral with its tower and cross so great that it does not afford gospel and grace to the poorest of the poor.

These stalwart men, who handle the ore and shape it for the market, are among the noblest specimens of the human race. They have busy brains and large hearts to match their brawniness of arm and giant grip of hand. They are the thorough men. Visitors, in looking through the mills, are sometimes inclined to pity the operatives as drudges, forcing in time for pay, and to consider such work degrading to manhood. The smoke and the grime of the business, to persons who are in the habit of judging men by surface indications, often deceive a casual observer. These iron-workers care but little for show; they hang out no feathery signs; they make no apologies for personal appearance; they are never ashamed of blackened faces, or singed and sooty garments. With bared breast and arms, they have a firmer tread and a more royal appearance among the flying cinders and circling sparks than kings who walk on marble floors, and conceal their emaciated bodies under the cover of regalia. Out through a rough exterior they show you an honest eye — index of a great heart, beating strong and well with the pulses of right living. Such men get the real sweetness out of bread, because they earn it; and the real refreshing out of sleep, because they deserve it. God pays the workingman a premium over and above his daily wages. Life to such men is dear, earnest, and full. There is more of heaven in the mills where these men work, and in the homes where these men rest, than in all the palaces of idle aristocracy the broad world over. They are producers, and not mere consumers. God never made a man and put fingers on his hands with the expectation that he should put them in his pockets, or in somebody else's pockets, and live like a leech, boring for others' blood, instead of making his own; and whenever men eat and wear more than they honestly earn, however showy and smart they may appear, they have the thief's remorse without the thief's excuse. Men with contented minds, pure hearts, and sound bodies are the happy men. The true nobility of this country do not bear titles, nor perpetuate greatness in the orthography of a name. They have their honor always warm and fresh in their busy blood; and it has unconscious perpetuation in the life-purposes and every-day habits of children and children's children.

The capitalist, too, has his place in the fraternity of toil. The man who invests his money in building mills, and vitalizing them with machinery, giving employment to laborers, managing vast financial economies, spending time and talent in providing implements for subduing the wilderness and making it to rejoice and blossom as the rose, is a public benefactor. He is tilling the soil, building homes, educating the masses, ornamenting the world, and may, in his line, be as much a prophet of God as an Elijah fed by the ravens, or a John the Baptist eating locusts and wild honey. It is such inventive and adventurous men that this world needs; and when their means are held for such use, and their minds absorbed in such utilitarian enterprise, their percentage of gain, even if large, is fair in this land of levels where the least may become the greatest. The church needs business-men as well as preachers — workers, indeed, rather more than talkers. The gospel has no controversy with the rich man whose conscience enlarges with his expanding purse. It censures only the covetous, the selfish — the man whose eye would spoil a neighbor's home to fill out some unrounded corner of his own possession — the man who starts up and half swears in his sleep at the possible unbottoming of iron safes — the man of wealth who seems hardly to possess anything but suspicion of his fellow-men — the man whose gains only serve as swallows of salt-water to his thirsty throat — the miser.

"There walks Judas, he who sold
Yesterday his Lord for gold;
Sold God's presence in his heart
For a proud step in the mart.
He hath dealt in flesh and blood;
At the bank his name is good;
At the bank — and *only* there —
'T is a marketable ware."

We have found a more satisfactory definition of Ezekiel's words amid the din and dust of a Pittsburgh rolling-mill and foundry than ever we did among the musty commentaries of the library. "As they gather silver, and brass, and iron, and lead, and tin, into the midst of the furnace, to blow the fire upon it; so will I gather you in mine anger and in my fury, and I will leave you there and melt you."

The first thing is to gather. These mills in Pennsylvania reach, by well-adjusted agencies, to the shores of Lake Superior, and to the mountains of Missouri for ore. It is gathered. But, as dug from the earth, it is mixed with worthless substance. The metal and the dross must be separated. This is done only by intense heat, refining and fusing the particles of ore, and consuming all else. The next operation after that of gathering is that of the blast furnace. Nothing but fire of intensely aggravated flame will dissolve the flinty partnership of centuries. This accomplished, the ore is first called metal. Still its form is crude and rough. It is, in this state, as useless as ever. It is nothing but so much uncomely avoirdupois. Its value is only in its possibilities. If this were the end, the material might as well have remained in the depths of the distant mines.

God, by the prophet, speaks of Israel as of metal mixed with dross. Men are easily alloyed. The favored people have become so earthly by long contact with mammon that they exhibit a bulk of worthless weight. The prophet shows by this figure how the Israelites have degenerated, from a state of comparative purity in David's time, to a condition of grossness which nothing milder than furnace-fire would correct. When the kingdom was divided, and human ambitions crept into the room of loyalty to heaven, the original head of gold became as arms of silver. But now, in the later day of Ezekiel, it has deteriorated into the darker and baser metal; and its ring and richness have become obscured. The prophet grades the people as brass, tin, iron, and lead — as much as to say: impudence, hypocrisy, cruelty, and stupidity. The religion of men had been well-nigh lost in the original clay from whence humanity sprang. But there is a good in all this rubbish which may yet be developed. The people, gross, scattered, and foreign, may be gathered into Jerusalem, the holy, central city. There is an appointed agency by which to reach and save that which is true, and to consume that which is false. The gathering of the people from the distances is like the gathering of various metals and ores with various percentages of dross, within a crucible, to be melted down and renatured, with all the recrement consumed by the process. They are in the city, besieged by hostile forces, swift and terrible as the winds. Jerusalem is one great blast-furnace: the wrath of Almighty God is let in upon the accumulated masses for their good. By the raging fire of persecution, self-esteem and sect-alloy are destroyed, mere human philosophies utterly dissolved, the rust and rubbish of ritualism blown away as ashes, and the inwardly pure and precious gems of truth made the more brilliant by the test. This seems to have been the teaching of the prophet; and history sanctions the inference. True it is, that Christians are always improved in temper by severe experience —

> "Like purest gold, that, tortured in the furnace,
> Comes out more bright, and brings forth all its weight."

The process that refines the genuine believer removes the dross - pretender out of sight. Such heats are necessities to purify the church. They are kindled in organizations and in individuals. They consume caste. They make smoke of fashion, and cinder of aristocracy. It is the way by which God destroys sin, and burnishes virtue. It is the only way to get at the true metal. The judgments of heaven are spoken of as "furnaces of affliction," and as "refiners' fires." This puts the sublimest meaning in the words of St. Paul,

"For we know that if our earthly house of this tabernacle were dissolved, we have a house not made with hands, eternal in the heavens;" and "we know that these light afflictions, which are but for a moment, shall work out for us a far more exceeding and eternal weight of glory!"

"Thus in God's furnaces are his people tried;
  Thrice happy they who to the end endure.
But who the fiery trial may abide?
  Who from the crucible come forth so pure
That Christ, whose eyes of flame the depths can span,
  May see His perfect image in the man?

"Not with an evanescent glimpse alone,
  As in that mirror the refiner's face;
But stamped with heaven's broad signet there be shown,
  Immanuel's features, full of truth and grace;
And round that seal of love this motto be:
  'Not for a moment—but *eternity!*'"

There is a Christian who has been prospered in business beyond his expectations. He becomes engrossed in the world for its own heavy sake. His heart begins to knit itself, fiber by fiber, to money, to estate, to position. Its pulse-blood beats out into carnal extremities to the sore chilling of the soul. He neglects his prayers at home to be in time at the exchange. He permits his Bible to accumulate dust, while his ledgers are posted and duplicated every day. Religion gets to be vague and vain — a matter of convenience or a nothing; and business is all and in all. Christ appears but a myth, and heaven a childhood's half-forgotten dream; while the bank becomes a shrine of devotion where the vows are paid in all weather, and the mill and store sufficient paradise. To this man there is more music in the rattle of iron wagoned to market over the cobbly streets than in the loftiest hymn of praise in Zion's courts. Christianity is alloyed with mammon. The old clay Adam gets the better of the new creature. The once heavenly-minded man becomes earthy, groveling and dull. But let the Bible tell it: "How is the fine gold become dim! How is the most fine gold changed! The stones of the sanctuary are poured out in the top of every street. The precious sons of Zion, comparable to fine gold, how are they esteemed as earthen pitchers, the work of the hands of the potter!" Sad indeed, when a man so neglects his Christ and his soul — when a church becomes worldly in its heart and compromising in its policy! Then God's way of renovating and renewing is by the flames. He saves men by fire. Let us heed well the lesson, and look to our privileges, our influences, and our solemn obligations. If we are sluggish and heavy, like lead; cruel and noisy, like iron; impertinent and proud, like brass; deceitful and glossy, like tin; corrupt and gross, like the wild ore of the mountains, God will kindle a flame of fury upon us and melt us into compacter and better substance, consume our follies, and reduce our boasted sects and selves to something useful and comely, though it be obscure and small.

> "Keen are the pangs
> Advancement often brings. To be secure,
> Be humble. To be happy, be content."

In visiting the mills you may have observed that the iron is hurried through the rollers while at white heat. As soon as the blue chill of the air begins to creep over it, the particles yield unwillingly to the pressure. The colder the iron, the harder to forge and shape. And so with men. The very best quality, as well as the worst, of human nature, is more susceptible to influence when warm. That is the time for impressions. Men in affliction — men made tender by sorrow and bereavement — men made responsive by courtesy and kindness — men made sympathetic by brotherly love — (for all these things are as coals of fire) — these are the men more easily Christianized than men tempered and cooled to ordinary atmospheres. If you would wield power over others, you must feel real interest in them; you must be able to impart warmth into their affections. If you introduce religion to persons who are cold, hard, and blue as flat iron in the warehouses — if you *strike* them with piety, as if you slung a sledge, you will most likely get nothing but resistance and clangor for your pains. God's Spirit alone can prepare the mind for truth; and it is the Christian's business to study circumstances, to watch for conditions, and to "strike while the iron is hot." But, as in iron-making, there must be gathering, and adjusting, and warming, with patience, and industry, and perseverance, before permanent results are secured. The Christian worker should be "instant, in season and out of season,"—awake and alert the whole year round. It is a lamentable state of affairs in the business world when the mills stand idle for weeks and months at a time. It is ominous of bankruptcy among capitalists, and of distress among the operatives. And so it is a subject of sorrow among the angels, when the church is intermittent and irregular in its operations. Many of our churches, active and efficient in the mid-winter, look all summer as if there were a strike among the members. The fires die out. The laborers lapse into indifference, and the work of salvation ceases. And this argues unanswerably in favor of Satan's kingdom: for suspension always precedes bankruptcy, poverty, and want. Not that we would discourage the most earnest efforts to save sinners do we thus speak, but to emphasize the fact that the New Testament churches are organized *to keep their methods moving always and everywhere.* Sermons, prayers, exhortations, and hallelujahs over returning prodigals, should sound on in ever-increasing tones until lost in the trumpet blasts of the judgment day.

In the process of casting iron in moulds, there are several conditions essential to success. A peculiar kind of sand is used, of certain moisture, grain, and temperature. In this the pattern leaves an exact impression of itself. Then when the metal is poured into the vacuum made by removing the pattern, there must be a way of escape for the air before the accumulating liquid. Without this precaution there would be a "blow," involving a loss of time and labor. Air must not occupy the room of iron. These unlike substances can not be forced into affinity. Sometimes such an invisible trifle as a puff of air destroys the largest casting. There must be vigilant attention given to every corner of the mould. With these conditions observed, there will be produced an exact imitation of the pattern. The character of the casting depends not only upon the model, but upon the manner of using it.

There is an apt illustration in this of the method by which Christianity is formed in individuals and in communities. Certain primary conditions are required. There is such a thing in the economy of grace as a *preparation* for the gospel in human hearts. The model of Jesus Christ, Son of Man and Son of God, must be there, with every feature imaged — the complete pattern of thought, and purpose, and life. The airy vanities of the world and empty ideals of the schools must be excluded. The likeness of Jesus in the soul can not be matured while any impediment is in the way. The divine Spirit must have free course to be glorified. There is a law in the gospel which forbids the coalescing of unlike principles in the human soul. A single clinging passion, or prejudice, or secret sin, would mar the beauty of holiness, and make worthless all attempted forms of religion. Christ and Beelzebub make no partnerships. They are as opposite in nature as metal and air. This is why so many half-in-earnest professors in the church, like ill-prepared receptacles at the foundry, blow out as fussy failures, and lie around the thresholds as rubbish until melted over again. Some religionists are moulded from the rough almost every year. The Prince of the Power of the Air interferes with many a conversion. He puts a clod of earth or a puff of air in the way of a man's spiritual development — a farm, a mansion, or a mill; a bank account, a bond, or a mortgage takes the room that belongs to God. Christ will have the whole heart or none. He is a perfect model of life. He must have imitation and affiliation in every feature, grace, and trait of character. The warm, loving heart conforms to Him. But the chill and harsh, the hard and haughty man is none of Christ's.

There is but *one* model for all Christians, of every age, and tribe, and tongue, in heaven and in earth, in time and in eternity, the same. Jesus, and Jesus only! The sects have human patterns. They mould men after Luther, Calvin, Wesley, and lesser and later models still. They patent the models, and cast the creed-brands in front places on human souls, as inventors do their names on metal wares.

There is incessant change of dogma, view, and opinion in theology, and these changes are formulated by doctors of divinity into patterns by which thinking freemen of God are to be cast and recast as so much running liquid! Converts are taken when warm in the love of God, and when ready to be Christians in and out and through and through, and run into Methodists, into Presbyterians, into Baptists, or into some other narrow shape, at great waste of soul and strength. Thenceforward, too often, by some strange chill, they are content with the lesser name than that of Christ, and with the smaller fraternity than that which girdles the immortal brotherhood of believers. The spirit which prevails in a sister church,* well named, if for no other excellence than this, "Christ's church," is the spirit of the gospel. Sinners are brought to the Saviour and permitted, and even advised, to select whatever branch of the church may be most congenial and convenient. Members of other denominations have been made happy at that

* This reference is to a Methodist Episcopal Church of large and active membership, under the pastoral charge of the Rev. J. A. Gray.

favored altar, and have gone back to their respective churches to work for the salvation of kindred souls. Wherever this charity obtains, the Kingdom of Heaven will be established. We do not disparage the ecclesiastical organizations. They are a necessary means. But they are not the end. Let them multiply and extend; but for the soul's sake and for Christ's sake, let them all conform to the image and will of Him who is all and in all, blessed forevermore. Let the denominations at least fit together like the various parts of an engine made by one common process, of one common material, cast separately, if need be, but to be supplemented, part to its counterpart, and keyed into one mighty agent, under God, for the overthrow of Satan and his kingdom, and not as so many distinct cannon, to turn their thundering mouths against each other in exterminating war.

If we must have the denominations, they ought to be brought into a tenderer and more helpful sympathy. They ought to be held together, if this be possible, in a more substantial unity. At no point and by no means ought there to be strife and friction between these "branches" of the family of Jesus. So should the love of Christ overcome all their differences of creed and diversities of mere opinion as to make them one at least in practical effort and constant purpose to save souls.

"Were love in these, the world's last doting years,
As frequent as the want of it appears,
The churches warmed, they would no longer hold
Such frozen figures, stiff as they are cold;
Relentless forms would lose their power, or cease,
And e'en the dipped and sprinkled live in peace;
Each heart would quit its prison in the breast,
And flow in free communion with the rest."

THE MACHINIST.

"I wisdom dwell with prudence, and find out knowledge of witty inventions."—PROVERBS viii. 12.

"O Lord, how manifold are thy works! in wisdom hast thou made them all: the earth is full of thy riches."—PSALM civ. 24.

CHAPTER V.

THE MACHINIST.

IF you were to visit a certain New England city, you would find, among many other interesting objects, a carpet-loom, so constructed as to weave a pattern composed of a dozen different colors, selecting and using the materials in exactly calculated proportions. As you watched the shuttles flying and the heddles dancing, it would seem as if the variously tinted threads were chosen and adjusted by the fingers of an intelligent being. The unerring certainty by which every shade of the woof is thrown into picture through the warp, would make it difficult to get rid of the impression that the supple-jointed iron were not endowed with thought. To me the spectacle was one of bewilderment and wonder. At first, the complexity of the thing was incomprehensible. And yet it was the invention of some brother human brain, and the workmanship of some kindred right hand in the race. Its plan and its particulars were soon apparent. Watching it weave for a while, its marvelousness gradually vanished. At first its designer appeared as a being almost great enough to be worshiped; but when the mind mastered the scope and use of the machine, the feeling was reduced to admiration and respect, for the loom was measurable by common finite understanding. The inventor was a genius, but his work was human. It might, any day, be superseded by another of greater capacity and elegance.

But how different our emotions when we come to study God's works in nature! Here is infinity, inviting investigation, and yet always stretching beyond our apprehension. God, as we have already contemplated him in these pages,* is a worker, shaping his purposes into tangible forms, for special results; but his designs and doings outrange our highest conceptions. The more our mental powers

* The Carpenter.

are elicited, and the more our experience is enlarged, the more does the field of possible knowledge expand, blooming, inviting, and beautiful before us. The larger our attainments, the less, relatively, do we seem to know. We see the evident marks of an Almighty intellect; but the great Original himself keeps evermore behind his handiwork, and appeals alone for love to our highest faculty—that of faith. His wisdom dwells with prudence. It solicits investigation; and the study gives men good heads and dextrous fingers. The Bible is a great incentive to all discovery. It has done more for true science than all the logic of worldly philosophy, policies of statesmanship, or victories of armies since the world began. The Scriptures record a progress of civilization by which the wilderness is made fruitful, deserts transformed into gardens, the elements of nature subdued and controlled, and the kingdom of darkness lighted up into the kingdom of God's Son. The church of Christ to-day, has the arts and sciences as her right-hand agencies of pioneering into remotest paganism. Printed

Bibles, locomotives, and lines of telegraph, are the new heralds of the Christianity which saves the masses.

From the Eden days until the time when Noah was instructed to build the ark, we have no account of any invention or handicraft by other than members of the family of Cain. The line of Seth is specially favored in chronology, the names, ages, and relations being kept distinct and definite. By this discrimination we have the data of the past, and may thereby trace the lineage of the Messiah. Any deviation from this peculiarity in the Sethite records is merely to note religious phases and hopes. But the Cainite registry is secular. This is why so many inventions are ascribed to wicked men. Cain, after his exile, built a city, and called it after his son Enoch. This implies a fact sometimes overlooked: that tent-life succeeded settled habitations. The Darwinian development theory finds a difficult problem here. The very first-born man in the race has designing genius. He builds a city. Tents had their origin several generations later. Builded cities antedate nomadic life by a thousand years. If there was a gradual progression it was backwards! Darwins, nor any other unscriptural speculators, are able, with all their show of learning, to explain the records of the primeval days. Human civilization has not been a growth out of a savage state. Eden was a paradise, and not a wilderness.

As to the style of architecture which characterized the first city, we can infer only crudeness and simplicity, for tools were few. Walls and roofs were put together principally with no other implements than the hands and feet. The first houses were necessarily plain and poor. They were erected for comfort rather than for ornament. Lamech, the fifth descendant from Cain, had two wives at the same time, and of course his troubles. But, withal, he had an inventive genius for poetry and music. Some sort of necessity, no doubt, aided his gift to practical results; for a man with two help-mates on his hands at once, would require a surplus of words and tones and winning ways to counteract domestic jars! "Necessity is the mother of invention," is a very ancient sentiment. Lamech's son, Tubal-Cain, inherited the talent, but turned it to more substantial uses. He was the famous inventor in works of brass and iron. Jubal, his half-brother, imitating the tact and taste of his father, discovered the art of giving musical sounds by instruments.

> "Jubal, the prince of song, (in youth unknown,)
> Retired to commune with his harp alone;
> For still he nursed it like a secret thought,
> Long-cherished, and to late perfection wrought—
> And still with cunning hand and curious ear,
> Enriched, ennobled, and enlarged its sphere,
> Till he had compassed in that magic round,
> A soul of harmony, a heaven of sound."

Whatever the extent of Tubal-Cain's inventions in metal, he stands as the first machinist in the annals of history. Some ancient nations even worshiped him under a name that signified "artificer in fire!"

The word machine applies to any instrument or organization by which power is made effective—to any thing, or system of things, by which specific results are accomplished. The primary object is to reduce the outlay of manual labor, and increase the amount of good to man. A machine may be composed of material parts, as in an engine; or it may consist of principles and laws, as in a code of government. The antediluvians had a knowledge of arts, and attained to degrees of considerable civilization. The workmen engaged by Noah built a large and eminently sea-worthy vessel; and such an enterprise implied tools and appliances of no mean order. The arts of useful life which were lost in the scattering of the tribes were gradually recovered. There were re-inventions under similar circumstances as those by which they were originated. For nation after nation rose and fell. Reverses in history have been hindrances to art. The darkest ages were not the earliest ages. Human nature waned by reason of idleness, indulgence, and passion. The sharp and disciplinary necessities of the primal days were life's best incentives. But later, by indolence, the blood of the race coagulated, and there was constant paralysis of power. We boast of this age of invention in which we live; we indulge the dream that there never was such a time — that there never breathed such a brilliant people as ourselves — that there never were such wonderful works wrought out by human hands as now. We may over-estimate the present because of our ignorance of the past. There are, away back beyond the midnight of the dark ages — beyond the frontispiece and blank pages of the world's popular history, — records and monuments of a civilization three and four thousand years old — of nations scarcely less advanced than our own. There were arts and economies then of which we are ignorant to-day. There were productions of beauty and utility which modern skill has not equaled, or approached. They who thought and worked out their designs in those days were conversant with laws in nature and in science, which are profound secrets to us. Indeed many of our most wonderful inventions are but revivals of old things of almost thirty centuries ago. And this makes stronger argument still against the "development theory" of Darwin and other popular philosophers. A very ancient Scripture tells it better than the most learned professor in any of the schools: "The thing that hath been is that which shall be; and that which is done is that which shall be done, and there is no new thing under the sun."

Sir Matthew Hale Smith, in his treatise on the Primitive Origination of Mankind, refers to this subject in these words: "We are not to conclude every new appearance of an art or a science is the first production of it; but, as they say of the river Tigris and some others, they sink into the ground, and keep a subterranean course, it may be for forty or fifty miles, and then break out above ground again, which is not so much a new river as the continuation and reappearance of the old: so, many times, it falls out with arts and sciences; though they have their non-appearance for some ages, and then seem first to discover themselves, where before they were not known, it is not so much the first production of the art as a transition, or at least a restitution, of what was either before in another or in the same country or people: and thus also it is said that guns and printing, though but lately discovered in Europe, were of far more ancient use in China."

It is a commendable trait in human nature, that no man desires to labor more than is necessary to accomplish his object. His constant and proper desire is to contrive means by which to economize physical exertion. A rich soil and a congenial climate are always esteemed as blessings, because people enjoy the results of industry in abundance rather than in pittance. A wise and prudent laborer wastes no strength that he can save. He works, not for work's sake merely, but to secure the largest possible results. Man is not the fool to wear himself out in such drudgery as beating the air, scratching the rocks, furrowing the sand. Labor without adequate compensation is regarded as a curse. Almost every human invention, from the first, has been designed to save labor and augment the sum of good livings for all. Horses, camels, and cattle have been made subservient to man — to bear burdens that would else have rested on his own shoulders — to draw the plow, which otherwise must have been forced through the sod by his own muscles. All nature is claimed, wherever it can be controlled, to subserve the same end. The creek turns round the wheel of the mill and grinds the grain, that, without such appliance, must have been crushed into flour by pebbles as pestles in weary hands. The wind is man's servant and does his work. A boat is an invention to save labor in transporting goods from place to place. Rowing the boat is less arduous than carrying its cargo. But to save the toil and fatigue of rowing, sails were invented, and the winds were harnessed to do the drudgery of man. To the same end the steam-engine was applied, and has become the mighty agent of doing in million-fold what the strongest combinations of men would fail in attempting to do.

Man is weak in body, frail of arm, short of life; and in a world where animals have greater strength of sinew and fleetness of foot, and are better armed both for attack and defence, than he, there is a divine fore-calculation concerning him, that he must invent. He must use his wits as the bird its wings. He invents tools, implements, weapons, agents, and nature bows a slave at his feet, conquered, controlled, and restless to do his bidding. There is a way for limited human power to grapple with and overcome physical superiors. Invention after invention makes him more powerful, more happy, more useful, more exalted in the scale of being. Man already more than flies. He sends his words as the fleet lightning round the world. The giant forces of machinery have revolutionized the world, and are hastening on the millennium as rapidly by days as once it could have come by centuries. The flint, and the bone, and the stone-hatchet of the savage in any age, the metal-edged tool of the mechanic, and the steam-engine of the manufacturer, — all have the same aim and purpose — to save labor and multiply comforts. It is a divine faculty imparted to man to invent and create, and to improve his productions to the end of time. The Bible itself has been made the common people's book by means of machinery; and missionaries of the cross are efficient and increasing in proportion as art and science are cultivated in lands already won to Christ. True religion sanctifies secular pursuits, and makes evangels of the dumb materials that have lain locked up in silence in mountains and rivers since the world began. All arts and scientific achievements among men are but the relics of an intellect defaced by sin. Like pieces of old coin, corroded with rust, we all bear the stamp of a royal Head. An Aristotle, and a Sir Isaac Newton were but rubbish of an Adam who stood sinless and at liberty in Eden.

Now this thought of invention for purposes of good in human affairs leads us to examine the system of things in nature by which we are surrounded and supported. We see marvelous ingenuity displayed in the elements of air, earth, and water, and in the movement of our planet along its place in the march of worlds. We see that the seasons are appointed and modified for specific results, by thc combined revolutions of other spheres, and by the adjustment of swinging systems of planets and suns in the firmament. To bring out a violet into bloom requires the united whirling of a million ponderous orbs. The universe is a machine, balanced in all its parts and counterparts to bless intelligent beings. God framed and fitted up the world, unrolled its grassy carpets, fringed its fields with flowers, spread out its silvery seas, reared its pillarless dome for the circling sun and glittering stars, — *finished* the creation of material things as a home for man, before he lifted him from the dust and breathed into his nostrils the breath of life. Man is not a mere accident or surplus of the creation — not the greatest because the last of the handiwork of the beginning. He was created a little lower than the angels. He was made to be maker. He has God's image and God's breath, and is immortal. For his body the earth was made; and for his soul the heaven of heavens. He may lift his thoughts to the skies, search out his Father, understand his works and his words, know him, love him, serve him, and live forever. The sweet singer of Israel long ages ago apprehended the scheme of creation in its beauty and bounty; and the One Hundred and Fourth Psalm is both a philosophy and a poem. Recounting the well-appointed order of nature by which every living thing is satisfied, and enraptured with the magnificence of the mechanism by which the seasons are re-volved and the wants of man supplied, he exclaims, "O Lord, how manifold are thy works! in wisdom hast thou made them all: the earth is full of thy riches!" God, the builder of homes for all his creatures, from the insect to the archangel, is also the benefactor of all. He feeds and clothes and equips the armies of heaven and earth.

From a vast and empty abyss where nothing was from all eternity, God commanded this wonderful creation to arise. It immediately came forth, as his infinite ideal, embodied, with harmony of parts, and perfection of purpose, and accuracy of movement,— shining and singing as a universe. How adorable is our God, "who clothes himself with light as with a garment, who stretches out the heavens like a vast pavilion, who makes the clouds his chariots, who walks upon the wings of the wind, who establishes the earth in its circuit," and wraps it round with oceans as with robes folded and fastened by rivers as with ribbons, a girdled pilgrim for its march in the company of obedient worlds!

The design and manufacture of an intricate machine by human brain and human hand are tedious and laborious, and often result in utter failure. There have been more failures than successes. The ruins of abortive inventions lie scattered everywhere, and among the ruins sometimes the brains of the unfortunate designer. But the production of the earth, sun, moon, and stars out of nothing cost the Almighty but a word. He spoke, and it was done. He commanded, and it stood fast. In an instant, as his will went forth, all things emerged from chaos into existence. The power of the Most High is absolute. He needs no aid from other powers, and the Omnipotence that creates a world can create a million universes, perfect and measureless as his infinite domain.

There are men of wealth and of office who glory in the power they sway over their fellow-creatures. They wear the insignia of royalty and bear titles of honor. They fancy themselves great and mighty. They rule nations, cast communities into formulated thoughts, habits, and fashions, and are revolved around by devotees like Saturn by its moons. They are not great by the power of genius; they are not the men who invent, who grasp real utilities, and create, and prosecute, and accomplish great measures for the reformation of the world. What are the grandest achievements of the best of men, compared with the works of God? What need has Jehovah for a Pope, a President, or a Peabody, as a supplement to his own manifested authority, power, and benevolence? Men may plan stately cathedrals, brilliant campaigns, unparalleled charities — may extend possessions, increase goods, gain applause — may be idolized as demi-gods on earth. Yet all this is but specious varnish, tinkling cymbal, empty chaos. The greatest of mortals use borrowed brains and borrowed muscles to execute their purposes. They are fed and clothed and housed by workingmen. But God does all his own work by his own right arm. He both designs and executes. He puts himself into the labor which embodies his purposes. It is not the divine method for one to invent and another to execute. Doing is equal in honor to thinking. The man who works out his own designs with his own hands works as God works.

The Almighty stood and measured the earth, says the prophet:* He looked and dissolved the nations. For strength and power are in his hands. He touched the trembling hills and they were wrapped in smoke; the ancient mountains burst in pieces; the rocks melted away like wax; the earth shook to its center, and the pillars of heaven were forced from their foundations. The sun and the moon stood still in their habitation: at the light of his arrows they went, and at the shining of his glittering spear.

St. John, in his Patmos rapture, heard a universal voice — the voice of every living creature in heaven, and earth, and sea, crying out in one accord, "Blessing, and honor, and glory, and power be unto him who sitteth upon the throne for ever and ever." "For

* Habakkuk iii.

great and wonderful are thy works, Lord God Omnipotent; just and true are thy ways, O king of saints! Who shall not fear thee and magnify thy name?"

He commands the light to go forth, and it goes, bounding along the horizons in silver sandals swifter than a fleet-footed hart on the mountains. He recalls it, and it obeys in the tremblings of eventide. The stars give light in their midnight watches, and sing. When they are called out as sentinels to keep vigil in the solemn silences, they answer, "Here we are!" This stupendous machine which God has erected is subordinate to his will in every atom of its substance. When the captives were led out of Egypt toward Canaan, the sea saw the approaching host and parted its billows before their weary feet. Before the children of God, Jordan rolled backward its currents and stood still. That the sons of Israel might prevail in battle, the sun halted in his march across the heavens. The Almighty touched the great orb with his finger, as a jeweler would touch the spring-wheel of a chronometer to drop a moment from its count.

He who created absolutely controls. The miracles of Jesus attest this truth.

"When God came down from heaven, the living God,
  What signs and wonders marked his stately way!
Brake out the winds in music where he trod;
  Shone o'er the heavens, a brighter, softer ray;
The dumb began to speak, the blind to see,
  And the lame leaped, and pain and darkness fled;
The mourner's sunken eye grew bright with glee,
  And from the tomb awoke the wondering dead."

You who appreciate the wisdom displayed in "witty inventions," and the genius and industry by which they are operated,—you who are convinced by the sight of a machine that it had a designer and moves for a specific purpose,—you can not but see that the same thought is enlarged and intensified in the creation around you, and of which you are a part. You believe in God the Father, Maker of heaven and earth. Will you also believe in his Son, Jesus Christ, by whom all things were made—the manifested God—the Immanuel—the Saviour of sinners? The infinite designer of the universe which you acknowledge to be perfect in all its purposes and parts, has a plan by which you may become immortal — by which all your sins may be pardoned, and your souls redeemed and exalted to the Divine Presence. The whole system of things around you is constituted with a view to your salvation. It comprehends the discipline and education of souls. It appeals to reasoning and responsible beings. The whole structure of man and the universe is interpreted by the Christ of God who died for sinners.

The divine character, like the pure light of day, is one uniform and unbroken mass of brilliancy. But the gospel is a prism, and by it we divide the rays; and we are surprised at their variety and beauty. We wonder how they should all so harmoniously unite. In Christ Jesus we see Justice and Mercy, Holiness and Truth — attributes of the Godhead — blended and perfected. By the plan of redemption, we see how the sinner can be justified, the law honored and magnified, and the divine government maintained. A God of infinite sanctity assumed the sinner's form and place that he might be capable of suffering in his stead; and that by suffering he might restore him to the inheritance which had been forfeited by transgression. The formation of the heavens had been but the work of his fingers; but in the work of redemption he made bare his omnipotent arm. By this he has broken down the gates of hell, and destroyed the kingdom of Satan. By the doctrine, death, and resurrection of Jesus Christ our Saviour, he has established a church as a refuge for all who believe in his name and are led by the Spirit. This is the religion which in the beginning was to the Jews scandal, to the Greeks foolishness, and to the Gentiles insignificance and obscurity. But in vain did persecution whet its sword to destroy it; in vain did rulers conspire and armies contend to hinder its growth. It prevailed by its own inherent purity against all the eloquence, passion, and prejudice of its enemies. It was divinely calculated and omnipotently worked, and nothing could withstand its power. It spread from Jordan to the sea, to the distant islands, and to the continents beyond. And now in every corner of the globe it has set up the triumphant standard of the cross. The kingdoms of the world are becoming the kingdoms of our Lord and of his Christ. It is an infinite design, omni-operatively executed, and its power must extend and accomplish what its Author intends, even the salvation of the world!

By his great power this vast universe began; and as soon as the course of ages which he has appointed shall be complete, by his power will it also end. Then every mark of worldly grandeur will be blotted out. The world and all its riches shall pass away. Let us make it our life-purpose to be great in heaven. To accept this free salvation is the only ambition worthy of an immortal soul.

THE POTTER.

"The precious sons of Zion, comparable to fine gold; how are they esteemed as earthen pitchers, the work of the hands of the potter!" —LAMENTATIONS iv. 2.

CHAPTER VI.

THE POTTER.

THE art of working in clay is of high antiquity. It ante-dates all other vocation and design. Adam himself was made of clay, his name *adamah*, the ground, implying his origin of dust. God imaged himself in an earthen vessel. It is a pre-historic thought and occupation. It is attributed by the oldest nations to the gods, or mythical personages. To the remotest references of Scripture, it is wonderful to find how often tradition has corroborating parallels.

In Egypt, the cradle-land of the arts and sciences, the god called Chnum is accredited with the invention of turning clay into vessels and ornaments by the use of finger and fire. In the ruins of some of the oldest structures ever erected in the Euphrates valleys and along the shores of the Nile, vases of red earthenware have been found. The sepulchers of the fourth and fifth dynasties have yielded evidence to the antiquity of the art by their brick-burnt pictures of potters at work.

Job uses the figure suggested by this art, when he speaks of his own creation as a work of skill and care: "Thine hands have made me and fashioned me together round about; yet thou dost destroy me. Remember, I beseech thee, that thou hast made me as the clay; and wilt thou bring me into dust again?" He argues that it would seem waste of work, after such pains and wisdom in one's creation, to be, by the same hand, dashed in pieces. For who would make a beautiful vase merely to break it when finished? Whenever this portion of the Bible may have been composed — and it is evidently one of the most ancient Scriptures — it has peculiar value and significance from its incidental notices of the arts and sciences as they prevailed in that distant time. The reference to man's creation as the work of a potter moulding clay, is frequent in the Bible. This seems to be an intentional use of metaphor, especially to recall the fact of Adam's origin, and to keep in remembrance a knowledge among all men, everywhere, of their bodily frailty and dissolution.

The Assyrians were extensively engaged in the finer works of clay. There were skillful potters among them who manufactured clay histories, mostly in hieroglyphics, clay title-deeds, clay documents of various descriptions for both public and private preservation. They wrought hexagonal prisms, cylindrical rolls, and different forms of registers for letters and statistics. Many of these were impressed with their official seals, burnt into the substance of the clay. About ten thousand fragments of an ancient terra-cotta library were discovered in a secret chamber of the palace at Kouyunjik. The history of Sennacherib's campaign against the Jews has been preserved by means of this indestructible process. Thoughts once cast and burnt into this adamantine material, are safer for after generations than when embalmed in hollow tradition, or inscribed on rolls of parchment. The potter's art was in full activity and highly developed before the fall of Nineveh, and was maintained as an occupation of honor and importance for many ages on the plains of Assyria.

The Babylonians, who immediately succeeded, and, in some measure, were contemporaneous with the Assyrians, shared the same customs to a large degree. They continued the art, turning it to essential uses in their temples and their tombs. They invented glazed coffins; and immense numbers of them were used. Some of these curiosities, in a state of preservation very remarkable, and containing handfuls of human dust, have been recently exhumed at Warka, and at Mugeyer, with other strange remains of the ancient days.

The Hebrews do not appear to have employed the art until after the exodus. They probably learned it in Egypt as a part of their bond-experience under the Pharaohs. Before that time they must have used other substances for drinking-vessels; or else procured them from other people. The very few Jewish vases now in existence do not seem to be older than the time of the Maccabees, although something of the art of glazing was certainly practised during the reign of Solomon. During the Captivity, the prophets frequently employed metaphors suggested by the potter's art, as, for example, in the passage quoted from the Lamentations of Jeremiah.

Until about 580 B. C., the temples of Greece were roofed with terra-cotta tiles, said to have been invented in Cyprus, and are formed similarly to the Roman, and are somewhat ornamental. These tiles, in many instances, have stamped upon them the name of the city, the potter, and the year of the emperor's reign in which they were made. Much valuable historical information has been preserved in this incidental manner, of vast value as corroborative testimony to the truth of the Sacred Scriptures. Many Bible proofs have been found among the ruins of pagan temples. God's Word has myriad witnesses, silent but eloquent, in nature and in art. And these tallying testimonies forever multiply as the past ages are explored and understood.

Friezes and other architectural ornaments, cornices, antefixes, pipes for draining, small figures of much beauty called pelina clays, and used for penates, or votive offerings, are among the relics of a remote day in Roman antiquity. In the ruins of Pompeii, drinking-cups of various ornate forms have been discovered; and although constructed of clay, they attest an ingenuity of workmanship which is admirable even now.

The potter's wheel, noticed by Homer at the beginning of the Grecian history, is probably a far eastern invention of earlier date. The wheel is described as a low, horizontal table turning on a central pivot, and made to revolve by an assistant, and was extensively used. It was constructed as a kind of lathe, for shaping vases, jars, and cups. The feet and handles of vases were stamped and moulded, while wet, to their respective places on the work. Some of these vases were made of the finest clay, and glazed and colored into objects of real beauty. They were sometimes elaborated into gods, and the trade became very lucrative. That region of the world is still famous for images as objects of worship, the relics of an idolatry which a corrupt Christianity has failed to obliterate.

The manufacture of pottery seems to have prevailed all over the habitable globe. Some of the finest productions are those of China. The very word, China, is indicative of the rarest earthenware in the market. It is fine, hard, light, and beautiful. Even in the heart of Africa the art is known, in Madagascar, and in the remotest islands of the sea. The aborigines of this country, probably Asiatic in their origin, have left specimens in their mounds similar in type to those found in the Old World. The monuments of the Aztec nations, so common in Mexico and in South America, show rare artistic merit, being, in many cases, decorated with the forms of deities, and occasionally covered with silicious glaze of great brilliancy. A few specimens have been found among the Aztec relics which resemble those of the Chinese. There is yet an unread history in these fragments of earthenware, that shall doubtless be worded into thrilling language and made to tell a won drous tale of the wandering tribes, and especially concerning the origin and object of the mysterious mounds of the Mississippi valley.

In England, potteries were operated as early as the time of Edward III., with indications that pitchers and costrels were made as far back as the eleventh century. There are relics of the ware that show pictures of the Norman knights of the reign of Henry II., and images contemporary with Edward II. The chief seat of modern English potteries is in Staffordshire, although at Fulham, Bristol, and Leeds, there are extensive works. Here, among the humble and industrious operatives, Methodism had rise and mighty power. It was in its beginning a religion for the working masses, simple, earnest, and efficient. And its success was that of the gospel, which at first and forever appeals to the common people.

"Like as a man Christ trod on earthly soil;
He bore each pang, and strove in every toil;
He spake with human words, with pity sighed;
Like us He mourned, and feared, and wept, and died.
Yet all the Father's fullness dwelt in Him,
In whom no shadow made the glory dim;

Such strength, O God, from Him to us derive,
And make, by life from Him, our death alive!"

But now, as in the prophet's days, and through deeper deliberation, there is sad backsliding from places of privilege and honor. Professors of religion, in attempting to climb to self-appointed exaltations, are often captured in the vain ambition, and thrown prostrate in the dust. The people, once warm in the love of God and fellow-souls, when unawake and forgetful, when inclined to the follies of sin and foot-set in the traps of Satan, lose their zeal, grow cold and callous, and are broken in an evil hour of passion as vessels of clay that are dashed upon the ground. "The precious sons of Zion, comparable to fine gold, how are they esteemed as earthen pitchers, the work of the hands of the potter!"

In the Hebrew this book of the Bible has no distinct title, but is named, as all the books of Moses are, from the first word, How? Jewish and Greek interpreters call it *kinoth*—Lamentations. Its composition is acrostical—a poem whose every stanza begins with a letter in the order of the Hebrew alphabet, as an aid to the memory in recitation. It was written as a kind of psalm for pious Jews, to console them in their sufferings, giving them accordant language by which to express their grief. And the poem is full of exquisite imagery. Even tears may be trained to flow in proper channels. Mourning for sin must have expression. Sorrow has its own rhetoric of sobs and sighs, and its tones of plaintive minor key. Jeremiah has been fitly called "the weeping prophet." The syllables of the simile sound as a piteous cry. The chapter opens with a doleful account of the change which had come over the inhabitants of Jerusalem. It is an elegy. The temple is laid waste. The glory of the city is departed. When the city was besieged and burnt, it was tarnished by the smoke; and the magnificent temple was thrown down among the rubbish. It had once glittered in the sunlight as a crystal gem on the brow of Moriah — a diamond on the mountain's crown which dazzled from afar like a day-star over the holy altars; but now its splendor is changed; its costly material is trampled in dishonor to the dust. The curiously-wrought stones of the sanctuary, so elaborate and skillful in their carvings, were thrown down by the Chaldeans, or shelved and riven by the scorching fires.

The princes, or priests, here called "the precious sons of Zion," were injured and abused. An enemy's hostility, accumulated and intense, had vent on their devoted heads. But, in the midst of distress, they have heavenly recognition. Sons of Zion! What a title of honor! How poetical and significant! Yet, under the proud oppressor's hand, how are the mighty fallen! The purity of hearts and the sanctity of souls are nothing in the eyes of wicked rulers. Although estimated by the inspired penman as fine gold, good men are accounted by the world as earthen pitchers. Men of truth, justice, benevolence — men of holy principles and noble purposes, are genuinely valuable. They have intrinsic worth. They are the salt of the earth — the light of the world. They are really great and rich, although apparently weak and poor. They are covenanted in sacred brotherhood; they are heirs of immortality. Angels are their servants. Jesus Christ is their Redeemer. Heaven is their home. For them the universe revolves its shining suns. All things are theirs. Believers of every name and nation are the precious sons of Zion, comparable to fine gold. They who are faithful have a name and a credit for Christ's sake, which are honored among the shining hosts above, although they may be often hungry, and hated, and hunted down on earth. In all ages God's people have been at discount in the marts of the world. Wealth mixes its alms with curses, and tosses the compound toward chill, shelterless pilgrims, as crusts and bones to a dog. The Old Testament saints were thus treated by peers of the realm and sons of estate. The first disciples of Jesus were ridiculed, mocked, and derided as the offscourings of the earth — as the followers of him who was hanged. The Redeemer himself appeared as a root out of a dry ground. He was despised and rejected of men. Down through the whole history of the church, good men have suffered persecution. The truest of men have been martyred for the cause so dear to their hearts. Even to-day the people of God are subject to relentless criticism and venomous contempt; and thrice blessed is he who endures it to the end—who, through cutting censure, and beating broadsides of opposition, presses his way forward to glory and to God! These tests are for discipline. They put armor on the soul. The virtues of Christianity as lived in men are this world's uplifting powers. And in these days of Satan's reign abroad, when the crowds are wading hellward in the miry clay, though Christians may be popularly considered as earthen pitchers, clay-modeled and brittle, as the work of the hands of the potter, still, bless God!—still and forever are they gold, fine gold, New Jerusalem currency, the precious sons of Zion! The world's opinion of Jesus and his followers is not the judgment-day decision. The haughty lips of men in ease, and bodily fat on good livings, may deride and disown the lowly Nazarene and his church; theologians may attempt to mould Christianity into convenient dogma and sect, ornamenting and glazing its front-surfaces, as a potter the clay; but the precious sons of Zion are gold and not clay, and they are not intended to be manipulated by human fingers, however skillful, into narrower form or fainter image than those of Jesus Christ.

God alone is sovereign over all people. But one is our Master, and all we are brethren. He delegates his power to no creature, not even to an archbishop or an archangel. There is no deputized authority committed to any being under or over the shining sun. Nothing that breathes the air or soars the skies has any commission to regulate the faith of men. There are ecclesiastical usurpers who deign to dictate certain finite and fixed opinions as creeds for believers. Young converts, susceptible to impression when their whole nature is softened by the Spirit of God — when ready to be renewed in the image of Jesus Christ and made free indeed by the emancipating powers of truth, are too often taken up professionally, as just so much senseless clay, trodden into proper consistency by the agony of repentance, to be put on the potter's wheel of Augsburg, Westminister, Andover, or some other local patent, turned into mere sectarians of specific form and feature, burnt into fore-ordained hardness and glaze, and fixed in statued discipleship, brittle and growthless as earthenware. There is an abundance of this plaster-of-Paris religion in Christendom. Protestants need not so criticise and ridicule the little images of Rome, until these specimens of cast formalism are removed from their own sanctuaries. They are shapes, and may be capable of sounds, but that is all. They occupy room, but exert no saving power on others. If they have spirit in them, they hold it as dumbly as jugs do their spirits. They stand as so much clay-work in the church of Christ. They do not, as intelligent and responsible beings, represent the gospel of grace as revealed in the New Testament — the broad, open liberty of divine sonship in Christ Jesus, original and alert as Pauls and Luthers and Wesleys for every new issue in discipleship. They are content with the empty forms of religion, while they deny the power. They are earthen pitchers, the work of the potter's hands. Not the gospel of the

Son of God, not the Holy Spirit, but treatises on theology have made them what they are. Custom has fashioned them, and not the blessed Christ. Many of our popular churches where the precious sons of Zion might have place and power, are nothing more than spiritual potteries where the sum and substance of all religion are run in clay, turned, baked and finished in fancy styles for exhibition. It is pretty, and so is a pitcher; and as a pitcher is hollow, so is this pious pottery of the churches. But the first blast of the judgment-bugles in the air will batter and scatter such earthenware to fragments. There is sad havoc made of souls when Zion's sons are degenerated to the dumbness and deadness of potter's work. The only test of true membership in the church of Christ is that recorded on the pages of the New Testament. The potters' wheels of later ages are human inventions to divide, confuse, and destroy the unity of Christian brotherhood. We do not urge objection to denominational organizations, if only they are sympathetic and supplementary in their methods. But when they become exclusive and belligerent, when they by common consent resolve themselves into heresy hunters, and use their breath and brains to magnify the letter that killeth, and in strife against the overflowing Spirit that giveth life,—when they become jealous of each other's spires and statistics, quarrel over each other's agencies, and proselyte from each other's ranks, they do excite in heaven the lamentations not only of sainted prophets, but of sinless angels, and the pity of the ascended Lord himself, "The precious sons of Zion, comparable to fine gold, how are they esteemed as earthen pitchers, the work of the hands of the potter!" Well, well indeed for us, were our weaknesses and worthlessness only imaginary, as in the case of the overpowered Hebrews. Their *enemies* so esteemed them; but in our bondage to time and sense, may not our *friends*, even our LORD, apply the same lamentation to us? Once there were shining sons of Zion in our now desponding and apathetic churches. The fine gold was here. But alas for the papery substitute! It is crumpled and soiled and torn! Once there resounded echoing hallelujahs on many a lip over the conversion of penitents at the sound of the glad tidings. Once there trickled fountains of tears within many hallowed walls—tears of joy at the victories of Jesus over Satan and his hosts. Once there was hearty co-operation in rescuing men from sin. Where are the precious sons of Zion now? Thank Heaven! they are beginning to shine again! The gold is coming into currency once more, an evidence that the divine administration shall stand forever. The rebels' sway is coming to an end. Satan retreats before the blood-wet banner of the cross. The dumb earthenware is being removed from the temple at last, the idols are crumbling down, and the genuine heart-worship is sending up incense and song to Almighty God again! There are new converts every day to Christianity. Believers are waking up to renewed diligence; backsliders are returning, and sinners are inquiring what they must do to be saved. United prayers have reached the Majesty on High, and down to the churches, in accordance with the people's faith, descend the answers in baptisms of love. To God be all the glory, as his alone is the power, and his the authority and dominion forever!

We have been asked to explain that famous passage in the ninth of Romans—those words which have been so often interpreted as an excuse for inaction and passivity in religion. But as there are secrets in the works, so are there secrets in the words of God, beyond our apprehension. They are the expressions of an apostle to a particular people; and letters often contain words susceptible of misconception by third or disconnected parties. We cannot, nor would we attempt to, grasp their meaning as isolated verses, much less to formulate a doctrine upon a casual metaphor. This is the reading: "Therefore hath he mercy on whom he will have mercy, and whom he will he hardeneth. Thou wilt say then unto me, Why doth he yet find fault? For who hath resisted his will? Nay, but O man, who art thou that replieth against God? Shall the thing formed say to him that formed it, Why hast thou made me thus? Hath not the potter power over the clay, of the same lump to make one vessel unto honor and another unto dishonor?"

But at the end of this same chapter, there is the great keyword of all grace — *whosoever*. In speaking of Christ, the apostle concludes, after all, that "*whosoever* believes on him shall not be ashamed." The teaching of the figure, as used by St. Paul, is to impress presumptuous men with the duty of unquestioning submission to God — entire acquiescence to his will in what he does for all. For the Almighty will not be climbed up to on any human-devised ladder. The way to him can not be paved with the rich man's gold; nor carpeted with the inventor's most gorgeous handiwork. In order to reach and rescue sinners as a common lump of humanity, God does not supplement himself with a pope, a bishop, a council, or a creed. Himself is in his Word, the same at once to all. He is no respecter of persons. The teaching puts us down into confession of utter helplessness; it takes pride and preferences out of our hearts as to methods of salvation. It is not empty capriciousness, for no such attribute is in the divine nature. It is not arbitrary persistence, without reference to results, for the whole Bible has an opposite import. It is an awful thing to mould an 'ism or a theology from fractional parts of chapters, to adjust eternal destinies from an apostle's paragraph, pen-pryed out of its place, and to preach a doctrine from disjointed syllables at variance with the life and gospel of Jesus Christ. Any apparent difficulty here is only as an intentional note of discord in an anthem of resounding harmonies. It is to start men into thought, thrill them into appreciation, move them into action; it is not to discourage or distress. There is an inherent and an irresistible drift of truth, which is the current of the New Testament, broad and sweeping and full. You have sometimes stood by the river-side and watched a backward-circling eddy near the rocks, where the water actually ran at cross angles, and against the course of the stream. You tossed in a leaf, and on the narrow current, it floated up stream, if you decided direction by the valley and general sweep of the river. But all the while the particles of water temporarily obstructed by the rocks, were sliding imperceptibly away into the wide river. The stream flowed downward surely and forever. To base a new theory of gravitation on the little impediment of eddy and whirl, and argue from it, that, because your dry leaf floated in a given direction, a certain definite quantity of the river, calculated to a drop from all eternity, did not run down stream, would be a vain delusion. And so to argue a mass of unsavable humanity from a sentence which may be negative in itself, but which is in deep and real harmony with the whole economy of grace, is a delusive theology. Jesus infinitely outmeasures Paul. The Saviour's message to the world is the river, even if Paul's whole epistle to the Romans is an eddy. Really the current is identical. On at the end of the rocky ninth of Romans, the eddy-drops of "whom—he—will" are free and aflow as one again in the blessed "whosoever;" and further on, at the close of Revelation, the still richer, sweeter, higher, broader, deeper "*whosoever will*," let him come to the river of life and drink, and drink, and drink till he is satisfied!

God, being the Maker and Ruler of all,

knows how to attain certain ends; and his procedures are necessarily beyond our comprehension. But we know that his tender mercies are over all his works. He is our Father, and he has a father's eye, a father's hand, and a father's heart. Our destiny is what we make it. Our happiness here and hereafter hinges on our own will. To the pure all things are pure. To the good all things are good. To the gloomy and base and bad, all things are bad and base and gloomy. The world about us is a great mass of materials, subject to experiment. We build our own character by will and work. By tact and time, the believer overcomes obstacles, solves problems, settles doubts; and it is God *chosen* into himself *by* himself, who shapes his destiny. There is a boundless universe spread out before us. To us there is offered the grandest possible opportunity for securing eternal life. Our only chance for heaven is in our hands. Our invitation to the skies is ringing in our soul for answer

"Listen, the Master beseecheth,
Calling each one by his name

His voice to each living heart reacheth,
  Its cheerfulest service to claim.

"Come to the good that is nighest;
  Dream not of glory afar;
That glory is nearest and highest,
  Which shines upon men where they are!"

THE GLASS-MAKER.

"Study to show thyself approved unto God, a workman that needeth not to be ashamed, rightly dividing the word of truth."—2 TIMOTHY ii. 15.

"And before the throne there was a sea of glass like unto crystal."— REVELATION iv. 6.

CHAPTER VII.

THE GLASS-MAKER.

THE time at which glass was invented is not known. There is a popular tradition that the discovery was accidental. Pliny has recorded the story of a few mariners who were transporting a cargo of nitrum, or, probably, soda, landing on the banks of the river Belus, a little stream that winds from the base of Mount Carmel, in Palestine. Finding no stones on which to support their cooking vessels, they placed under them some masses of nitrum, with which the region abounded; and when the fire became well kindled, they observed that the nitrum melted and fused with the sand into a liquid and transparent stream. This has been a current account of the origin of glass.

The ancient Egyptians, however, were certainly acquainted with the art of glass-making. Earthenware beads have been found in old mummy cases, having an external coat of glass. Among the ruins at Thebes fragments of colored glass have been exhumed. There are strong arguments adduced to prove that the art of glass-making was practised in Egypt before the exodus, giving it a chronology of five-and-thirty hundred years. It is evident that the manufacture of glass was known in Alexandria, and had been introduced into Italy, Spain, and other countries, before the time of Pliny, who records the Belus River theory of its origin. Utensils and ornaments of glass have been found in the ruins of Herculaneum. At Warka, in Mesopotamia, in the ancient mounds, are strata of baked clay coffins to the depth of forty feet, and within these quiet recesses of the dead, which have been undisturbed for thirty centuries, are found relics of gold, silver, copper, and glass. At Nineveh, in a subterranean chamber of a palace, were discovered bowls of glass, covered with pearly scales with veins of brilliant opal variously tinted under different lights. Beneath the accumulated *débris* of ages in other ruins of that city was also found a small bottle, bearing the title of the Assyrian king, Sargon, in cuneiform characters, and a miniature image of a lion's head. This would fix the date somewhere about seven hundred years before the Christian era. There is no reliable information that transparent glass was known at any earlier period.

It is generally believed that the first glass-houses, or manufactories for turning the ware into market, were erected in the city of Tyre. There were peculiar advantages for glass-making and for transportation at that point; and Tyre was for ages the center of the commerce in this staple. Thence the trade extended to Rome; and during the reign of Tiberius, there were whole streets of glass factories there, although the art seems, at that time, to have been employed almost exclusively in producing articles of luxury. Only the wealthy Romans and their foreign equals could afford the indulgence of such elegant wares. It was probably in Nero's time that clear crystal glass was first produced. Thitherto the specimens had been more or less opaque. The first transparent glass was an object of great wonder and admiration, and was celebrated by the poets in enthusiastic rhythm and rhetoric. Horace* and Virgil refer to the beautiful creation of crystal in language rivaling in luster the theme of their song. One of them compares the beautiful substance to the waters of the romantic Fucine Lake glittering under the Italian sky.

The decline of the art in Rome is succeeded by its introduction and prosperity in more northern cities, especially in Murano and Venice. From its establishment here and in Bohemia, its progress can be traced to Germany, France, Britain, and to the United States. From its success in Venice, where the most exquisite

* Horace, in his Odes, Book iii., Ode 13, uses the simile. The following translation of the passage, by Dr. R. Audley Browne, is a faithful rendering:

"O fountain of Blandusia, more brilliant than glass,
Worthy of sweet wine, not without flowers,
To-morrow I will present thee with a kid
Whose forehead, swollen with its earliest horns,
Both love and battle foretokens
In vain——"

cups and goblets were produced, the art became honorable above the ordinary trades, and operatives were permitted to mingle with the royal families, and even to marry the daughters of noblemen, a privilege conferred upon no other mechanics. It is not uncommon in foreign lands, even to this day, to trace the flow of kingly blood down through the veins of glass-blowers. In France, it is said, several distinguished families are sprung from this class of tradesmen, some of whom have been honored with the highest dignities and offices.

It was about the year 1557 when glass-manufacturing was introduced into England, where it made but slow progress for a hundred years or more. In 1700, the English Government granted substantial aid to the business, and from that time Venice of the south, had a rival in the island of the northern seas.

The application of glass to windows is of comparatively modern times. In the year 674, foreign artists from the continent were employed to glaze the church windows at Weremouth, in Durham, England; and so late as

1567, this mode of excluding cold and admitting light by the same medium was confined to the aristocracy. Until near 1670 the use of window-glass in Scotland was so limited that only the front and upper rooms in royal palaces were furnished with it, the rear and lower apertures having wooden shutters. But, gradually, since that time, the Scottish people have received light, until now every humble home to the remotest Highlands has its window-pane and lamp. Many a cotter, now, has

"His wee bit ingle, blinkin' bonnilie,
His clean hearth-stane, his thrifty wifie's smile:
The lisping infant prattling on his knee,
Does a' his weary, carking cares beguile,
An' makes him quite forget his labor and his toil."

The introduction of glass-making into the United States was a few years prior to the Revolution, and was attempted by a company of Germans at Quincy, Massachusetts. Their specimens were rude and limited. Then in Brooklyn, New York, and in the forests of New Hampshire, works were erected. In 1820 a New England company began a similar enterprise in Kensington, near Philadelphia, but disagreement between the proprietors and workmen soon defeated the project. In 1808 a few glass-blowers from an abandoned manufactory in Maryland, reached Pittsburgh, and were engaged by one Col. O'Hara in the erection and working of the first window-glass factory west of the Allegheny Mountains. In Geneva, and at other points on the Monongahela, like establishments followed; but the great center is in Pittsburgh and immediate vicinity, there being at present, according to statistics furnished by Mr. Atterbury, twenty-four firms or factories engaged in the production of flint or crystal glass, besides about as many more that turn out window-glass, jars, vases, and other articles. The facilities for coal, together with the natural avenues of commerce, doubtless contributed, as in the iron trade, to the location of these important works in this place. The history of this department of industry would, if written, reveal much of interest and influence in making Pittsburgh the great city it is. There were many failures, disappointments, experiments and losses, before the trade became secure. But now it ranks next to the first in the several staple productions of the place.

Here are thousands of workingmen of kindred tastes, temptations, and habits, who are worthy the special attention of the churches. If Christians do not take an interest in their occupation, they can not be expected to take an interest in Christianity. If glass-blowers as a class are outside the churches, it is because church-members have kept outside of the manufactories. If they are ignorant of the plan of salvation, it is because we are ignorant of their plan of workday life and labor. But there are devoted Christians among the working masses, notwithstanding the apathy and indifference of the churches. The gospel workman must have something for this large class of mechanics that is in the line of their own thought and vocation,—must study to make himself acquainted with the history, relations, and specialties of their business, so that he may rightly divide the word of truth, making most of its elements, as they make glass of given materials—giving to each a portion.

The analogies in this department of thought and labor are many and significant. Illustrations of Christian life and duty may be crystallized from the common facts in glass-making into lenses that reveal the Saviour to sinful men.

The first instance where the word glass occurs in the Bible is in Exodus xxxviii. 8, as a syllable in the translation of a word which might be rendered *mirrors*. In our version it is *looking-glasses*, and refers to articles in common use by the women. These mirrors were plates of burnished brass, capable of casting reflections much clearer and sharper than those from polished silver. It was not a vain habit to consult the looking-glass, but a religious rite among the Egyptians; for all the women, as they approached the temple, were tastefully adorned, and carried a musical instrument in the right hand and a mirror in the left. It is a custom among Arab women to this day to carry their mirrors with them as a part of their apparel. The laver for the priests to wash in was made of the women's looking-glasses. Females, in those early days, who assembled at the door of the tabernacle, were willing to sacrifice all else to devotion. This is an honorable record for the sex who have been, through all the ages and aspects of the church, the more frequent, devout, and earnest at shrines of worship. The women both of the Old and the New Testament times are the examples of faithfulness in religious service. In the tabernacle days they assembled in troops, ready to part with their ornaments and sacrifice their conveniences for the blessedness of acceptable worship. Rather than that the workmen should need brass, they would contribute their looking-glasses. The toilet should be desolate, that the sanctuary might be beautiful. It was, in honor, preferring the Lord's house to the home-parlor. The record itself is a mirror for us all. In these days the church gets only the fragments of our time — only the nickels and crumpled currency of our dollars—only the remnants of our thought and life — only the easy hours of fair weather attention. Business absorbs all else. Churches may be mortgaged; Sunday-schools suffer for air, light, and books; missionaries starve and shiver in heathen lands, if only oil and wine may flow freely at domestic feasts. A splendid mansion, and a dashing carriage, broadcloth, satin, gold, diamonds, and cologne for one's self, and nothing but crusts and crumbs for Christ! This old looking-glass in Exodus is not so dim after all!

The language in the book of Job is of similar import, in which Elihu, speaking of the sky, compares it to a molten looking-glass — a great, suspended mirror formed by fire and mould. The early notion of the firmament accounted it as a broad, solid expanse, reared as a dome over the heads of men, fixed on mystic pillars to stand forever. The Bible accommodates its language to the apprehension of the people; but it no where makes an assertion which science will not attest. We speak of the rising and the setting of the sun; and yet we know that such terms are but relatively true. The object of the Bible is primarily to teach religion; but it every where suggests and encourages scientific investigation. For God's works and words agree. The sacred writers used the popular phraseologies, just as philosophers do now. The fact that this dark earth contains the elements, that, when combined, make glass the only medium by which the eye can explore the firmament,—and that every sweep of the telescope but reveals higher and grander beauties still, is, in itself, a challenge to scan the universe of worlds. We find eyes in the clods by which we may read the poetry of the stars. Men may, by the skill of their fingers, supplement the power of their own vision, and lift a lens between themselves and heaven which opens a million marvelous creations beyond this little planet on which we stand and gaze; or, reversed, show a million wonders more in the universe of animalculæ below. The sky is indeed a mirror, and so is every drop of water, reflecting the handiwork of God. The deeper we penetrate the mysterious recesses of nature, the more profound our discoveries, and the more satisfying the evidence that our Father's house is one of many mansions, as Jesus said. Here in the flesh, and standing on this plain of graves, peering through the tears of sense and the dust of time,—we do see "as in a glass darkly." But, some day, the veils shall be rent, the clouds dispelled, and the blinding tears all wiped away; some day we shall have an outlook from the sunny summits in glory, and shall see face to face, pierce the secrets of eternity, and know as we are known.

The ingredients that enter into glass,— sand, soda, lime, niter, and arsenic,—are all opaque in their raw condition; but when melted and fused, become, in the partnership, clear as crystal. The particles when isolated and separate, are dull and gross, but all the while have hidden affinities which combine under certain conditions into a mass of brilliancy and beauty. Science discovers these secrets, and industry works them into practical results. The Creator of all things furnishes the material with given possibilities, imparts to man the inquiring spirit and the applying tact and forces, and stimulates him to accomplish by toil and patience what otherwise would seem as the direct work of his own almighty hand. God has built the world for a workshop, and not for a dwelling-place. It is stowed with materials and with tools to be taken hold of by men's hands and used. There are beckonings to study and to business in the rocks, in the sands, in the plants, in every thing; and every human hand is jointed and sinewed for work. The dumb beasts have no use for the gospel or for science; no capacity to enjoy the one, nor any faculties to experiment with the other. They are provided for by another economy. But man, imaged in the likeness of his Maker, is himself a producer; his brain and hand are the agents of a power which even angels may not exercise. Man as an individual, rather than as a race, is progressive, and the wide world is his laboratory.

The church, if composed of but one element, would be opaque. The variety of human character is what makes the real unity in a company of believers. Soda alone, or lime alone, never makes glass. To attempt a method of bringing men to one gauge of thought as a test of membership, is as unwise as for a glassmaker to spend all his capital in sand. There is the same result in blending unlike traits and dissimilar souls, as in bringing glass out of its individually uninviting elements — the crystal of true communion. The church, to shine, must embody all types of humanity, rich and poor, learned and illiterate, old and young. And a nation, to be transparent and beautiful as a whole, must recognize in its organization, as constituent parts, all gauges of stature, all shades of color in hair and skin, all brogues of tongue, and all keys of voice. In the church and in the nation, the unlike elements produce the crystal completeness, as in the composition of glass. The sand needs the lime, and both need the soda, the niter, and the arsenic. Poison itself loses its deadliness in the partnership. And so does the true church attract, absorb, use, and crystallize even the worst of sinners, who, if left in outer isolation, are death-dealing in every breath and act.

In a glass-manufactory the principal object is the furnace where the pots are set for the melting and fusing of the essential materials. Everything radiates from this center. The flinty broth is gathered on the point of a hollow rod, swung in the air by studied balancings, and blown into specific form by the operator's breath. All this is done with dexterity and vigilance, the most elaborate shapes being wrought out in a few seconds; and the small hand's-size of original liquid chills into a crystal vase, or pitcher, or other form, by the outer air. The endless variety of shapes and styles of ware is met by the busy workmen who dip the red masses on the points of their blow-irons from the boiling-pots, and swing, breathe, press, and cut them into forms as many and as exquisite as fastidious taste can ask.

And all these utilities and beauties are wrought out of dull and obscure materials, that lie as common rubbish beneath our feet! The fire subdues and fuses, and busy fingers and daily breath transform the bulk into a thousand elegant designs. This illustrates still further the thought of Christ's church as a kind of crystal palace, where all varieties of originally dull, dark, heavy, and even vicious humanity, fused by the fires of God's own kindling into common mass, are so touched together in these elements which are immortal, that by contact they become luminous and symmetrical. Thus may it be with the denominations of Christendom. Isolated and alone they are opaque bodies; but when brought into contact and sympathy, when their self-nature is melted, they flow into a spiritual compact which is infinitely brighter and better, the one true, radiant church of believers.

The sincere minister of the gospel recognizes this fact in his office and work, and labors not so much to enlarge and intensify a sect or an opinion, as to build up the broad kingdom of the Son of God. He does not so much care to accumulate the mere sand, soda, and lime of Christianity, as to fuse all the factors of truth into a blessed unit. He studies to show himself a workman that needeth not to be ashamed. He does not put material into an east wall which he has stealthily pried out of equally important position in the west wall. He rightly divides the *word* of truth that the *spirit* of truth may be unifold and full. He discovers, discriminates, compares, adjusts; he brings unlike materials into complementary completeness, and out of varied types of thought, and feeling, and life, by the fusing influences of the Holy Spirit; he aims to establish in the lives of men a Christianity which is open and clear as the day, seen through and admired by all, and in substance, though so transparent, is yet as firm and enduring as the glass that holds all its atoms, and shines with uncorrupted luster through centuries of time. And as a vessel of glass is the same in transparency every where, in one use as in another, in window, or vase, or pavement, or coffin, so is a Christian transparent under all circumstances, in places of honor, and in places of reproach, at home, abroad, in office, in prison, at a wedding, and at a funeral — always the same. He is known by all men by the crystalline consistency of his life.

"Religion pure,
Unchanged in spirit, though its forms and codes
Wear myriad modes,
Contains all creeds within its mighty span,
The love of God, displayed in love of man."

"Religion's ray no clouds obscure,
But o'er the Christian soul

It sends a radiance calm and pure,
  Though tempests round it roll;
His heart may break with sorrow's stroke,
  But to its latest thrill,
Like diamonds shining when they 're broke,
  Religion lights it still."

In glass manufacture there is a process called *annealing*, which especially interests the visitor. Glass, on suddenly cooling, acquires great brittleness. A chill, after the most pains-taking and successful moulding of vase or goblet, would cause the beautiful structure to fly to pieces. A slight touch of finger-nail or crumb of glass has, in a critical moment, sometimes crushed the finest specimen of artistry to dust. There is a remedy for this tendency in new-made glass. By annealing, or reheating the ware, to a degree a little below that by which it was melted, and gradually removing it from hot to cooler temperatures, the particles are toughened into more reliable affinity. A circular train of cars, on wheels made for slow rather than rapid movement, in the establishment which I visited, bears hundreds of fresh-blown vessels in easy advances out from hot to ordinary temperature, in a kind of graduated oven, and this simple process occupies a thousand-fold more time than the shaping of the articles. This brittleness of the glass is attributable to the disturbance of hasty cooling in the arrangement of its delicate particles. There must be deliberation in its adjustment to the new state.

This may serve as an illustration of the brittleness of new converts. They will not stand rough handling. A single thoughtless word has ruined many a young Christian. After conversion, they must be annealed. They must be trained into strength to resist the ordinary temptations of life. Conversion is not enough. By prayer and patience the new convert must be disciplined to daily duty, advanced by careful degrees into Christian work, and come by time and regularity into strength.

And there are some old Christians who have never been annealed. They may have been converted years ago, but not being needed particularly, being more ornamental than useful, they have, like blown but unannealed glass-ware, been on the shelf and hidden. Their names are on the church register, and that is about their greatest achievement in religion. They are never in use. They have become so accustomed to the shelf and the shade, that you never miss them. They keep in rear places and dark corners. They have the form of Christianity; they may have tone enough to pray; they may look solemn and behave respectably in their distant retreats—may even say "our church," "our minister," "our doctrines." But all the while they have never been annealed. A sudden temptation and their temper flies. Invite them to the prayer-meeting, ask them for missionary money, suggest a few hours' earnest work for Jesus, and snap! they go to pieces! They may have been converted, but they were put on the shelf before they were annealed, and they are worthless ware. It is possible at any time, and even probable, on a bright Sabbath morning, that a gentle touch from the pulpit on the subject of personal consecration and work, may crush some of these tender vessels of the church to fragments! I have seen so slight a thing as a bit of wooden pencil, dropped from the hand into an unannealed glass goblet on the workman's table, shiver it to atoms. But no matter how long a piece of glass-ware has lain idle and unnoticed on the shelf, it may still be annealed as easily as a new-blown specimen warm from the maker's hand. The two may pass through the oven side by side, and emerge together as equals for the test of use. And this is what all the churches need—that their crystally clear and prematurely cold professors should be put into discipline, into exercise, into self-denial, into sacrifice, into endurance for Christ's sake for a season, and gradually tempered into practical religious work; and then the gospel would have power on the minds and hearts of sinners. Every church ought to have its annealing apparatus, and keep it turning until every brittle vessel of the Lord is tempered into reasonable discipleship.

For this is a life of work, of trial, of tears and fears, of conflicts fierce and long. Christianity is both thought and action. The truth must not only be rightly divided as to language; in men's lives there must be consistency, symmetry, patience, workmanship in deed. But after all our toils are done, all our sorrows ended, we shall, if faithful, be permitted to mount up, and survey, and enjoy for ever what St. John on Patmos so faintly saw, — the city of our God, whose pavements are as sapphire and as a sea of glass clear as crystal. There our vision will be perfect. There the hearts as the faces of all will stand clearly revealed. We shall see as we are seen, and know as we are known, when we tread the ether plains before the throne. The sea of crystal is emblematical of the purity of heaven, where all weary workers for Jesus shall rest and rejoice. I can not explain these glorious words of the exile looking home. The vision was a rapture to him; and his record is a thrill and a song for us. The measure of the apostle's meaning, or the Spirit's message, we may not apprchend. But some day we shall know it all. The words mean revelation by and by. What we know not now we shall know hereafter. A man unable to look up and see the blazing sun in the heavens, might be able to look down and form some idea of its brilliancy and beauty by looking at its image on a placid lake. So Christ and the high heaven in which he shines are too great for our mental vision to apprehend, too profound for mightiest telescopes to trace. But in this quiet mirror-verse of the New Testament we catch a glimpse of the supernal glory. We would rather sing it than explain it—rather wait than wonder! What an anthem for the soul!—"And I saw, as it were, a sea of glass, mingled with fire: and them that had gotten the victory stand on the sea of glass, having the harps of God. And they sing the song of Moses and the Lamb, saying, Great and marvelous are thy works, Lord God Almighty; just and true are thy ways, thou King of saints!"

"And the city had no need of the sun, neither of the moon, to shine in it: for the glory of God did lighten it, and the Lamb is the light thereof! And the nations of them that are saved shall walk in the light of it: and the kings of the earth do bring their glory and honor into it. And the gates of it shall not be shut at all by day, for there shall be no night there."

"Ah, here we grope and stumble through the chill
encircling gloom,
The few sweet stars that cheer us, lighting only to the
tomb.
We try to trace His footsteps on through maze and mys-
tery,
And follow in our blindness, trusting where we can not
see;
But in yonder crystal radiance, ever welling from the
throne,
We shall see Him in his beauty, and know as we are
known."

THE PILOT.

"Behold, I send an angel before thee, to keep thee in the way, and to bring thee into the place which I have prepared." — EXODUS xxii. 20.

"Thy wise men, O Tyrus, that were in thee, were thy pilots." — EZEKIEL xxvii. 8.

CHAPTER VIII.

THE PILOT.

IN maritime countries the term pilot is used to indicate an officer in a ship who has general charge of the helm, and gives exclusive attention to the ship's course. The word also applies to a person who undertakes special charge of a vessel, to guide it in particular rivers, roads, or channels, on entering or leaving ports, and who assumes peculiar responsibilities aside from those of captain or master, in consequence of his special education or qualifications in the field to which his duty is restricted.

In some countries pilots are established for particular ranges of coast, and maintained as servants of the government; and a master of any ship engaged in foreign trade must put his vessel in their hands, in both outward and homeward voyages. There are regulated laws of pilotage, systems of training, rules for license, qualifications for fraternity, with charitable provision for superannuated pilots. Such association in all professions and pursuits is commendable. There is a deep-natured sympathy among men of the same vocation; and when it enlists the hand with the heart, the fellowship has bounty and blessing in its bonds. Trades' unions for mutual improvement and protection are worthy of encouragement.

The art of navigation had new impetus, indeed a revolution, in the invention of the mariner's compass, — a magnetic needle, balanced on a pivot, which by some secret law in nature always points to the north. This little instrument was found to be a reliable index in all seasons and under all circumstances, and became the key that unlocked the vast regions of the sea, and by which unknown islands and continents were opened to mankind. The knowledge of magnetic power as a directive agent was a secret to the early centuries of the world. Even the Greeks and Romans, in their scholastic times, failed to apply this natural principle to commercial purposes. It was not until late in the twelfth century that European nations brought it into use as a guide upon the trackless ocean. The compass, however, has been known and used among the Chinese, in India, and in Arabia, from periods of remote antiquity. The annals of these heathen empires show this to have been one of the many evidences of a high civilization before the Christian era. The earliest Jesuit missionaries to China, not likely, for manifest reasons, to report any brightness or beauty in idolatrous lands without strictest examination, agree in the conviction, and publish it to the world, that the Orientals are entitled to the invention of the compass, at a date some 2600 years before Christ. A translator from the Chinese authorities speaks of the origin of the compass as "a chariot for indicating the south, in order to distinguish the four cardinal points." The Chinese, however, did not apply the discovery to navigation until about the year 265 after Christ. Thereafter we find scattered references, in their public records, to ships directed over the wide waters by the needle. The compass was known on the Syrian coast before it came into use in Europe. For ages it was guarded with jealousy by the nations possessing it as of special commercial importance.

In 1260, Marco Polo, it is said, returning from his travels in the far east, brought back to Europe, among many other Chinese inventions, a knowledge of the compass; and about the close of the fifteenth century, another explorer found his way around the Cape of Good Hope, piloted by the sea-charts and needles of East India origin.

It is believed that the use of the compass was known as early as the close of the eleventh century in Norway, and was employed for purposes of navigation; for at that time there was no lode-stone in the northern countries.

Different nations and various ages claim the honor of this invention; but there is no claim so well authenticated as that of the Chinese, our far eastern rivals in courtesy and skill, now so scorned by political Christianity as they greet us from the west. Strange and cruel that the people who gave us the secret of the seas,—who pointed out by their genius, long ages ago, our broad continent of privilege and plenty,—should now, in these days of schools, churches, and republicanism, be treated as dogs rather than as men, when they land upon our sunset shores!

By means of the compass the earth's treasure-depths have been discovered, cities located, states mapped out, and lines of railway made to weave into unity the diverse nationalities of all the earth. It is the silent, but safe and unerring pilot of civilization, and occupies a prominence in the secular and religious worlds accorded to no other contrivance of human hands. Not only the mysterious seas, but the broader firmaments of sky, as well as kingdoms, empires, republics, commonwealths, farms, fields, and dwellings, are mapped and memoried by the aid of the pilot's needle.

The prophet accredits wisdom to the Tyrus pilots. "Thy *wise* men, O Tyrus, were thy pilots." Tyre was situated at the entrance of the sea, with many commodious harbors. Standing at the head of the Mediterranean, it was a center for trade through a populous country beyond. Occupying a position between Greece and Asia, it became a metropolis of merchants and the emporium for ships of every sail. The Tyrians were among the early navigators, and developed the art as fully as it could be without the use of the magnetic needle. Their ships were stoutly built and elegantly furnished, having the best of fir-wood, oak, and cedar timbers, and ivory for benches and ornaments. The sails were of fine linen, woven in Egypt, and richly embroidered. The state-rooms were hung with royal purple and finest tapestry. The oarsmen were specimens of physical strength and endurance; and the pilots were men of culture and skill. The owners of the Tyrian trading-vessels gave high wages for competent labor, and their voyages were, consequently, prosperous and pleasant. What these people of Tyre did in ship-building and cruising, they did well. It was thorough work,—a business that enlisted their best talent, means, and energies.

Thus should every occupation in which men

engage enlist their ablest powers. All secular employment, to be enjoyed and to be successful, must be heartily pursued. Whatever is worth the doing at all, is worth doing well. Be it managing a ship of state, or a ship of trade, a mill, a farm, a mine, a store, a wagon, a pen, or a spade, drudgery can be taken out of it whenever the heart is put into it. Wise men were the Tyrus pilots. They made their business a study. They ennobled the art into a science. They contributed to the dignity and good reputation of the city by diligence in their special line of business. So can all work be made honorable. The Bible allows no slovenliness in business. Christianity encourages invention, promotes refinement, suggests method, insists upon order, promptness, regularity, good humor, good manners, and good livings. The resources of the earth are abundant for all. If manual labor were made a part of education — an essential in every school and college curriculum — the world would be brighter and cheerier for the change. It is because labor has been dunned out as toll for a livelihood — underpaid, overtaxed, unfashioned, and unchurched, that so many toilers are worn, and weary, and forced to be illiterate and melancholy; whereas, if their work and position were properly rewarded, they would be strong, vigorous, intellectual, religious, and happy.

"The smallest bark on life's tumultuous ocean,
  Will leave a track behind for evermore;
The lightest wave of influence set in motion,
  Extends and widens to the eternal shore;
  We should be wary then who go before
A myriad yet to be; and we should take
  Our bearings carefully, where breakers roar
And fearful tempests gather; one mistake
May wreck unnumbered barks that follow in our wake."

On our river steamboats the office of pilot is one of highest honor and greatest responsibility on board. The pilot must know the channel in all stages of water, the precise location of rocks, bars, and snags; he must keep himself informed of every change in the depth and drift of the current. And this knowledge must be available by day and by night; for not only valuable cargoes of freight, but human life also is involved in faithfulness of the hand at the pilot's wheel. It will be recollected what a dreadful casualty occurred not long ago on the Ohio, between Cincinnati and Louisville, when two magnificent steamers, unskillfully guided, came in collision, and were destroyed, at the sacrifice of many lives. A slight turn of the pilot's wheel neglected or wrongly done, or the too feeble sound of a signal at the touch of his foot — a very little thing in itself—was probably the cause of that double disaster. Of all men, the pilot should be a man of wisdom.

When a man has a long journey to make through a forest or unknown region of country, through which he has never traveled before, he selects a careful guide, and engages his services for the way. He trusts in the wisdom of another — commits to his keeping his treasures and his life; and under the direction of a competent guide he safely reaches his destination at last. When a vessel is to cross or cruise along the seas, a pilot who knows the dangers of the route, who understands the winds and the currents, the geography of the distant shores, the location of the obstructions that lie hidden under the waves, is employed to take the wheel and move the helm. Special wisdom is sought and trusted for the voyage.

Human life is a voyage. There are dangers all along the way. The channel for safe sailing winds among rocks and over reefs, and often the perils are difficult to see. There are contrary winds and counter-currents to drift the soul away. Man needs a pilot. He is in jeopardy every hour. He is without knowledge of the breadth and sweep of the heady seas. He can not span the dim distances before him, nor make the harbor of which he dreams as lying calm and quiet in the open sunlight by the other shore. He has no compass by which to trace his way from time over into eternity, and be sure of his reckoning, pressing on in light and dark the same. But God knows man's low and lost condition. The Creator is a pitying Father, and proffers help to all the ruined race.

The promise quoted from the Book is from the lips of God himself. The children of Israel, human-natured and exposed, need the guidance of a special power. They are to be led forward by a hand which moves at the will of Him who sees the end from the beginning. An eye that never sleeps, down-looking through all storm and night, sees a way of deliverance for an obedient and a patient people. The pathway through the wilderness shall be pointed out even to the promised land. An angel is the pilot. He is especially qualified for the work of advancing the bewildered hosts, helpless and hopeless without celestial aid. This beckoning angel, at whose hand the multitudes press onward through heavy marches and tedious wastes, is no other than the Son of God, the same who, ages afterward, led the little band of disciples up and down Judea's rugged walks, until from Olivet he was parted from them in a cloud. It was the Angel of the Covenant, the Messenger of God, the Light of the World, the Way, the Truth, and the Life. He now, as then, and to us as to the Hebrews, goes before to keep his people in the heavenly way, and to bring them to the place which he has prepared. "I go to prepare a place for you," he said. "Come hither; *follow me;* I would have you where I am." Jesus Christ who descended from heaven to meet and rescue sinful man, has again ascended to the throne. To and fro he has traveled the way, from Paradise to Golgotha and back again. He is the wisdom as well as the power of God. Humanity's Pilot is heaven's King. He knows the dangerous shoals, the quicksands, the hidden rocks along the deep, for he has made the voyage himself. He, as man, was tempted in every point, as we are tempted. He is touched with a feeling for our infirmities. But he is absolute Master of the sea and storm, and has Death and the grave put under his feet.

Although the Divine Redeemer is unseen by our natural eyes, he guides men by the promised Spirit. Conscience is the believer's compass. Our future safety depends upon our fidelity to the dictates of this monitor within the breast. By heeding conscience men learn their special work and power. How often we hear persons complain of the monotony of life! They have surplus time hanging over their heads, and they study means to kill it. By games, by stupid novels, by stupider dress-parties, by stupidest conversation, all in befevered adjectives from fashion's limited vocabulary, stale and senseless as the clatter of machinery, aimless and useless people try to kill time, and escape conscience and the judgment.

The meanest insect under our feet has a mission, and fills a purpose. Not a plant, or blade of grass, or leaf, but what has in nature its appointed place. Is man an aimless being? Is man the floating waif on the sea of time? The trouble with many persons arises from the fact that they are drifting about without a pilot, moved on every current and wafted by every wind, passively on, as a mass of innate material, to certain wreck and ruin. When time hangs heavy and life is dull, it is evidence that men have not discovered the tendencies within themselves, that they fail to apprehend the purpose of their own creation, and are living without an object. The compass is obscured, the pilot's hand is palsied, and the helm is astray.

Now, to ascertain one's own nature and possibilities, the tides and currents of the sea of life, and the hither boundary of the eternal lands, intelligence was imparted to man. Conscience is the guide to the soul's safe harbor, and as the agent by which the Holy Spirit operates upon the mind. God speaks the soundings, and forewarns of peril and gathering storm through the conscience, as a pilot from his high outlook at the wheel speaks through the winding trumpet-tube to the engineer below.

And as a pilot takes real pleasure in the duties of his post from hour to hour and league to league, enjoying the advance he makes in the face of contending elements, so does the Christian bless himself by daily consecration to his common work. Heaven is not altogether external and distant. It is heaven already to every soul that is fronted thitherward in openness and light. Some painters have represented heaven as a company of little round-cheeked chubby cherubs blowing silver bugles, or as an ether loft among the stars, where pious people sit in silent circles all around, and are exceedingly happy because of their exalted position.

But there is a heaven in which to attain the heaven of heavens. As a well-built and elegantly furnished vessel in which to cross the seas is inviting, and even luxurious, so is the church of Jesus Christ, instituted at his command and piloted by his almighty arm, a delightful transport from the shores of time to the shores of eternity.

A man with noble purpose and living faith makes his own heaven in the association of true believers. The blessed kingdom is not so much a change of position as a change of self. The idea is practical to the man of business, the workingman, the mechanic, the merchant, the handler of needle, or spade, or wheel—you must trade, legislate, invent, dig, strike, act in every thing with a design to bring heaven down to earth. When once you discover your gift and place in the world, take the wheel as a pilot, hold to the indicated course against wind, current, and tide; for when you move in God's will, crooked places become straight and rough ways plain at your feet. This takes dullness out of life, and gives it cutting edge. This banishes monotony and melancholy, and puts courage, cheer, and glory in the heart. This makes the years golden-winged and beautiful as they fly. This makes a man wish for days of a hundred hours, and for a score of hands instead of two. And if men can not so put themselves into their work, and make ordinary vocations radiant with religion — if parlors and kitchens are not sacred as sanctuary altars and Christly as cathedrals, there is reason for suspicion that the pilot is asleep at his post, and that life is drifting to destruction.

It is a custom among some rich men to have the door of the safe where their money is deposited so arranged that, on opening it, a signal-bell is made to ring an alarm in their sleeping chamber; and a thief in attempting to steal by night may not reach the coveted treasure without giving warning to the owner. In some such way God has adjusted the conscience as a signal-bell to sound an alarm whenever Satan attempts to force an entrance to the soul. There is timely warning given. There is no sleeping-time excuse for losing the heavenly riches which are treasured in a

Christian's heart. So long as a man continues faithful to this unerring monitor, he is invincible to the attacks of sin. As individuals, men are accountable for the heed they give to this faithful sentinel within the breast.

One dull and dreamy August evening, a few years since, I was a passenger on board a steamer on a northern lake, bound for a port on the coast of Canada. All day long a haze had filled the atmosphere; the sun seemed, as it went down over the western banks, like a ball of copper sinking in the ground; and a dense fog crept up from the surface of the waters, and wrapped the vessel like a heavy veil. The distant shores had been but faintly visible under the noonday sun; but now, at eventide, the objects on our steamer's deck but a few steps from us were scarcely discernible. The fog and smoke shrouded in mist our fellow-travelers with whom we face to face conversed. We were approaching the port, and doubtless other vessels were near us on the lake; but the strong signal lights failed to penetrate the gloom. The night intensified the darkness and the danger. There was imminent peril. Collision and wreck would be but the work of a moment in the awful calm and blindness of such an hour. Hark! Faintly and from afar comes the muffled toll of a bell. We happened to be standing near the pilot. He looked as though he had heard the bell from the beginning of the darkness. He had caught the familiar tones long before we heard the tolling through the heavy air. Toll! again. Silence and anxiety, and again the tolling tone of the bell. It is louder and we — hark! — the bell — we are nearer — the bell. It is the fog-bell sounding from the shore. Suddenly there looms up the ghost of a ship; we are almost upon her; but the pilot saw the vessel before we did, and clears her safely. Other ships appear and disappear like specters in the gloom. The bell continues to toll; the pilot signals to the engineer below; the ponderous wheels again reduce their speed; the vessel moves more slowly still; the variously colored lights from land begin to glimmer through the gloom; and on past ships at anchor and ships afloat, on past projecting headlands and massive piers, our gallant steamer is rounded gracefully in to the landing, and we step out upon the solid wharf and street.

So the heavenly Pilot guides the ship of Zion through the gloom. We are passengers, happy in the cheery cabins and state-rooms of the vessel, anxious only when we step out to the bow or up to the decks and try to peer through the mists to the unseen shore. But One is at the helm who knows the waters well, and whose hand will guide the vessel through. We doubt sometimes, and fear, and find fault, and wish we were safe over the treacherous sea. But while we are trembling and afraid, hark to the tone of the fog-bell sounding from the shore! "This is the way!" "Come hither!" "Hold fast!" "Be thou faithful unto death!" "Lo! I am with you always, even to the end of the world."

"Friends, fondly cherished, have passed on before:
Waiting they watch me approaching the shore;
Singing to cheer me through death's chilling gloom,
'Joyfully, joyfully, haste to thy home.'

Sounds of sweet melody fall on my ear:
Harps of the blessed, your voices I hear—
Rings with the harmony heaven's high dome,
'Joyfully, joyfully, safely at home.'"

What blessed encouragement, when the earthly horizons disappear, when the helps of men all fail, when we are absolutely dependent on another arm for deliverance, to rely on Him who is mighty to save! When the Christian can no longer see Jesus, he can hear his voice, and feel the uplifting power of his arm. Though thick darkness settle over the soul, the sound of the fog-bell may be heard—the voice of the Spirit—still and small as a muffled note, and it is sweet to the heart. "Follow thou me." "Whosoever will, let him come! *Come!* COME!"

Conscience answers to the beckoning bell from the heavenly shore. If we heed the signals we shall at last step from these swimming decks and from this perilous gloom, out to the streets of crystal and gold, and tread forever the solid floors of our Father's house of many mansions.

That was a brave and noble pilot, who some years ago, on Lake Erie, when the steamer was discovered to be on fire, near half a score of miles from shore, turned her bow to the nearest land, and stood at his post until the flames wrapped him round in lurid light. The passengers were frantic with alarm. The officers were bewildered by the tumult. But his eye was fixed through blaze and smoke upon the land, and he stood firm at the helm until the garments fell in cinders from his body. "John Brainard," cried the captain from below, "can you hold on five minutes longer?" "I'll try, sir," was the reply. He stood there determined to die at his post rather than attempt to save himself at the peril of the passengers. He clung to the wheel until his sinews crackled, and the bones of his right arm were laid bare by the fire, and then with foot and left arm held the ship ashore, and perished in his place, just as the rescued people leaped from the wreck to the land. Who does not honor such a hero? Who would not trust in such a man? His was a greater achievement than that of

Wellington at Waterloo — greater than any victory that carnal conqueror ever won.

Yet this is but a feeble illustration of what Jesus Christ has done to rescue an imperiled race. He came to deliver the world from sin and the second death. He assumed a suffering nature that he might die. He gave his life for men. He died, the just for the unjust, — hated, scourged, mocked, taunted, and tormented to the last by powers in authority, and by thoughtless multitudes, for whom, by his very death, he made salvation free. He was slain for us.

Sinner, Jesus voluntarily suffered death for you, that you might live forever. Why do you hesitate to trust one so wise, so merciful, and so good? You who guide our steamboats so safely on the rivers, aiding our commerce and earning honor and reward, — you who have great vessels so completely under control, and to whom are committed precious human lives in utmost confidence — are you yourselves drifting without guidance to the grave and out into a shoreless eternity? Are your souls afloat on the currents that sweep downward forever? Have you no knowledge of this chart that maps the celestial landing? Are you willing to be accounted as so much dumb and dead material, when God would lead you to heavenly places in Christ Jesus? Let the suffering Lord of glory possess your faculties and your affections, kindle your consciences, and direct your thoughts, and you will find such strength and enjoy such liberty as you never dreamed it possible for dying men to share.

O what a failure, if, after all your years of successful piloting, never even perhaps to lose a barge committed to your care, you should at last be utterly wrecked yourselves — stranded in the river of death, broken and scattered as fragments along the dismal depths of perdition! Be wise men, O pilots, and heed the tones that echo in promise from the eternal shore, the words of God struggling through the heavy mists to arrest your attention now, "Behold, I send an angel before thee, to keep thee in the way, and to bring thee into the place which I have prepared."

THE PRINTER.

"O that my words were now written! O that they were printed in a book!" —JOB XIX. 23.

CHAPTER IX.

THE PRINTER.

THE word "printed," in the ancient Scripture, means *engraved;* for the art of printing was unknown in those days. Job had a creed which held his head and his heart, and he desired to perpetuate it as something more substantial than a tradition. It should be more than merely chalk-marked on the rock; he wished it cut to the granite's heart, that the crumbling centuries might not erase it forever. Arabia has many inscriptions on the mountain rocks to-day. Who knows but that, in some sequestered place, Job's creed will yet be found and read? It would be a simple one, but sublime; it would be central of all humble, patient, holy purpose, and superior to all the dogmas that modern theologists have compiled and foisted on the churches.

The old patriarch would transform rocks into Bibles on which future generations might read, for all the coming years, the doctrines that were sacred to his soul. A true creed is self-expressive. It struggles for utterance in every honest heart. It cries for syllables on the tongue, and for record on the monuments of time. Jeremiah felt it as a fire shut up in his bones. Peter and Paul were so inspired with the gospel that they could not but preach. Truth glories in expression. Faith must well up and run over into words and works. Job said, as the substance of things hoped for, "I know, *I know* that my Redeemer liveth, and that he shall stand at the latter day upon the earth;" that the good news — the glad tidings — should ultimately spread and fill the earth as the waters the channels of the sea. These words of faith in the world's Redeemer have been perpetuated, printed in a book, and multiplied in hundreds of languages to millions of people.

"Stars are poor books, and oftentimes do miss;
This book of stars lights to eternal bliss."

Men in a savage condition have always been without an alphabet. Ability to write by means of letters is a mark of civilization. Before any characters, as the elemental signs of sound and thought, were invented, the memory of important events was preserved by heaps of stones, as the Bethel of Jacob in the wilderness; by planting trees; by instituting festivals; or by historical songs. The first attempt at communicating ideas to others through the eye, was by means of paintings. The Egyptians used certain symbols called hieroglyphics — sacred carvings — grouping several things in one picture. It was a crude and indistinct method of conveying either fact or fancy, but the world knew none better. The Phœnicians invented letters, and Cadmus introduced them into Greece some 1500 years before the Christian era; but his primitive alphabet was limited, containing only sixteen letters, although it was afterward extended by Palamades and Simonides to twenty-four.

Most of the ancient writings were on stones or bricks. The Ten Commandments were thus inscribed. Afterward, plates of brass, of lead, of earthenware, and blocks of wood, were used. On these, for many ages, all public records were kept. At first only capital letters were known, as is proved from old marble monuments and antiquarian coins.

Then the liber, or inner bark of trees, came into use; and hence the name *liber*—a book, and library—a collection of books. Afterward linen and wax-covered tables, parchment, or the skin of animals; and next, in the time of Alexander the Great, a fabric began to be manufactured from an Egyptian plant called *papyrus*, from which the word paper is derived.

The instrument used for writing was an iron-pointed pencil, called a *graphium*. The Romans wrote on but one side of the parchment or paper, and attached the end of one sheet to another, and when the work was finished, it was rolled on a staff or cylinder; hence the word *volumen*—a scroll. The term volume, to us, suggests an object square and with angles and corners, rather than round, as a roll.

Julius Cæsar introduced the custom of dividing the continuous scroll into pages, and folding them in convenient measures with the folios marked as at present. In writing letters the Romans always put their own name first, then the name of the person addressed, with any expression of esteem and affection they chose, and forwarded their letters by special messengers, or commonly by slaves; for there were no mails or post-offices. Some of these incidents of correspondence are discernible in the introductions and postscripts of the New Testament epistles.

But even by this tedious process books accumulated. Solomon, in his day, said, "of making many books there is no end." Ptolemy Philadelphus collected at Alexandria, 274 B. C., a library of 700,000 volumes. This famous library was destroyed by fire from Cæsar's fleet, again restored to almost its original dimensions, and totally destroyed by the Saracens in A. D. 642. Augustus founded a Greek and Latin library in Apollo's temple on Palatine Hill; others were collected in the Capitol, and in the house of Tiberius, besides private libraries of rare value; and all this literature before the art of printing was known in book-making.

The world's annals, poems, and pictures were all in hieroglyphics, tombs, coins, and cumbrous manuscripts, until three-fourths of the time from Christ to us had lapsed away.

Printing is the art of producing copies of writings or other marks by means of pressure. Any substance that will receive an impression by reason of its softness, as wax or clay, or of its bibulous nature, is susceptible of receiving color from some pigment with which the stamp is moistened. Strictly speaking, however, the copies produced are not *fac similes*, but are reversed; yet the relation of the print to the type is always perfectly assignable, so that any form may be given to the result by means of the stamp.

The use of engraved seals for impressing soft substances, preceded by many centuries the art of printing by transference of a pigment, that is to say, by means of colored stamps or types. Indentation of properly conditioned surfaces was practiced in very early times. A common foot-track in the sand could not fail to give hint of the art.

Copper-plate printing, or the art of word and

object-grooving in hard substances, and thus making hollows for the ink, and then pressing the sheet upon the plate to absorb the color, is a custom of earlier practice than that of printing from types. This contrivance was invented in China by a minister of state named Foong-taon, and is still in common use in that country. The page of writing to be reproduced is pasted down over the smooth block, generally of pear-tree wood, where it leaves its letters and other characters in an inverted form. The wooden surface thus marked is made ready for printing from, by cutting away all the uncolored part of the wood, leaving the impressed lines in bold relief, ready to receive the ink from the brush or roller for impressing copies. The Chinese language being complex and arbitrary as to its alphabet, having an unmanageable conglomeration of characters, not reducible by laws of orthography, this block-page process, or half-hieroglyphic style of printing, is about all that the Chinese brains and fingers could ever make of the art. An alphabetical mode of writing, where letters represent elementary sounds instead of ideas and things, is essential to the full development of printing.

Even in Europe, where writing was from regulated alphabets, the Chinese mode of printing was the first practiced. It is credibly recorded that Marco Polo, who returned from China about the close of the thirteenth century, brought with him some specimens of paper money stamped with a seal covered with vermilion. The first samples of printing in Europe were playing-cards, and manuals of religion, a variety at the beginning which has been observed ever since, the Devil and the Lord having a divided interest in the art. Genius will always promote error as readily as truth, unless controlled by sovereign grace. Talent turns to the cause of Satan or of God, just as the heart elects.

The age of these crude block-prints was the first half of the fifteenth century. One still in preservation in Lord Spencer's library in England, bears the date 1423. Of the block-books, a small folio of forty leaves, each leaf containing a picture and a text of Scripture, published somewhere between 1430 and 1450, a copy is now in the British Museum. Another block-book was a small Latin Grammar for schools, issued in those innocent days before the era of book agents, committeemen, and morocco-bound voting!

At this point, printing would surely have stopped, if the art of alphabetic writing had not been adopted. The word-method, or block-page system, was impracticable for the infinite combinations of thought. The art must be based on individual letters, and be made to modulate from the simplest elements of speech. All possible words and sentences, from homeliest prose to sublimest poetry, may be wrought from a simple alphabet; and if a sufficient number of types, consisting each of but a single letter, be provided, and the same types used in printing one page afterward distributed and reset in other words for the next page or form, the new principle is found to be practicable at once; and from its application we date the origin of printing.

The employment of moulded types, and the manufacture of these types by casting in metal, were the organic changes from the Chinese system which made printing what it is to-day. That wonderful instrument, the alphabet, being already invented, this improvement from logography, or cut-wood and block-page printing, consisted in simply breaking up the wooden block into as many distinct pieces as there were letters engraved upon it, and by moulding the letters in matrices instead of engraving them by hand. The casting of metal types was only a separate department of the founder's art, which, as we have already seen, was one of the vocations of antiquity.

To Laurens Koster, of Härlem, belongs, according to reliable and impartial history, the honor of inventing and using movable types.* The Germans, owing to a social or political prejudice against the Dutch, have well nigh succeeded in appropriating to themselves the discovery of the art of printing, while, really, they have only developed and popular-

* The art seemed to have been locked up in his rude chase as a sacred secret, and it was not until others either supplemented or reproduced the invention, under other auspices, that printing found favor and became practicable.

ized what had its origin in Holland. But, all claims aside, printing was not so much a discovery by original genius, as it was an inevitable consequence of gradual increase of knowledge. There were thinkers in those days, and a necessity had come for putting ideas broadly before the people. Paper had been already invented, and xylographic or block-books were common, and it remained only to make movable types to perfect the art. So the credit scarcely belongs to one individual, or to a single nation, of furnishing the world the means of "making books without end."

In the year 1426, Koster first applied ink to adjustable wooden types, and in ten years after, a system of metal types was successfully adopted.

About the year A. D. 1442, John Guttenberg, of Strasburg, in Germany, improved upon the practice of printing from adjustable blocks of wood, and succeeded in producing some specimen pages in good style. He contended with many difficulties, working in secret and alone for a time, and was, at last, about to abandon the enterprise in despair, when he formed an intimacy with John Faust, a wealthy citizen of Mainz, to whom he confided his plans. Faust, himself an ingenious mechanic, became at once interested in the new process, and furnished means to carry forward the work. Soon afterward, Peter Schoffer, of Gernsheim, was also identified with the invention, and these three German workmen stand side by side in the honor of having established this noblest of arts. Their sturdy, full-bearded faces are grouped in the popular medallion which printers everywhere recognize as the badge of the craft. They had some personal misunderstanding, and even litigation; but all these local troubles are long since forgotten in the grateful memory of what they accomplished for the world.

From this date forward, printing became one of the most important and influential arts; and the history of its development and application is one of rare interest throughout civilization. It assumed an unexpected power in moulding thought and controlling governments, such as no other single agent had ever exerted. And this influence increased with every age, until now the press is the great lever by which communities and nations are moved into enlightened action.

If Solomon, who, when books were so tediously made, thought there was no end to the business — if, when every letter on every page was traced by a pen in weary, aching fingers, he had occasion to be astonished at the numerous volumes which resulted — what would he say, and how he would stare at a modern power-press tossing off, as mere child's play, its twenty-five thousand sheets in an hour! What kind of interjections would he pronounce when convinced that a single morning will rush into the market all over the land, ten thousand fresh books complete and beautiful for ready reading!

The first printing-press in North America was set up in Cambridge, Massachusetts, in 1639, a few years after the settlement of the pilgrims. There had been a press in operation, however, at Lima, in South America, from the year 1621. In both these instances, the primary object was to promote religion in the western world — the northern press by the

Puritans, and the southern by the Jesuit missionaries. It is not difficult to determine which has had the greater success. It is believed that printing was practiced in Mexico as early as 1569; and specimen copies of small devotional works are said to be still in existence which bear the imprint of the Spanish missions there near that time. But by some strange incubus, ecclesiastical or political, the press has never, in South America or in Mexico, accomplished what it has done in the British colonies and the United States. Where the Bible has been free, paper not unreasonably taxed, and conscience untrammeled by priestcraft or party, printing has been both pioneer and harvest-gatherer of Christianity.

The first newspaper published in America was in Boston, bearing the date of Monday, April 24, 1704, and called the *News-Letter;* the second was the *New England Gazette;* and the third the Philadelphia *Mercury*. The third periodical in New England was the Boston *Courier*, James Franklin's paper, and on this journal, Benjamin Franklin, the younger brother, served his apprenticeship among the types. The printing-office was to him more than the college has been to thousands of youths born, bred, and booked in the luxury of later days. He honored the trade, and the trade honored him. Sometimes we hear the remark from unmannerly graduates and fastidious fools: "A printer! nothing but a printer! O but printing is a mean occupation!" The charge is false. No honest vocation is mean; and this has special attractions and delights. By its peculiar discipline, it made the boy Benjamin Franklin, a profound philosopher; the boy, Horace Greeley, a conscientious and powerful politician; and the boy, Thomas Hewlings Stockton, the pulpit orator of his day. It is a noble employment. It develops talent. It encourages genius. There is a charm in the touch of types that is magnetic. I had rather spend an hour in a printing-office among sprightly workmen than an equal time any where else in search of general information. The business makes men ready thinkers and correct talkers — barring the bad grammar of occasional profanity, which is always evidence of an awkward printer — and if employers would treat typos as artizans and equals, and provide respectable offices, and proper and ample materials, printing might take its legitimate place as first among the trades — as a calling of peculiar dignity and honor. A printing-office ought to be as neat and winsome as a school of design among artists. If printers would keep themselves in "good sorts" socially, as they like their cases to be literally, this glorious art would come out of its drudgery, and be sustained by just appreciation in the form of good wages, genial associations, and airy and wholesome hours and apartments.

But, supposing that we are in an ordinary printing-office, let us make some observations and draw some inferences as we go along. A type-setter is called a compositor. He works at a sort of desk, known as a stand, the surface of which is divided into two inclinations, the nearer portion to his hand being called the lower case, and the further and steeper portion the upper case. These two cases, with corresponding ones for italics, contain all the letters, small and capital, figures, marks, points, and spaces arranged in boxes or open divisions, according to their frequency in words, the most used sorts being nearest the hand. Hence the small letters are in the lower case, and capitals in the upper case. The spaces, or blank types, by which words are separated and lines adjusted in the composing-stick, are also arranged in boxes according to their thickness. From these cases, letter by letter, the pages of books and newspapers are made up. Here the manuscript, or "copy," placed in the printer's hands for reproduction, is transferred to the solid squares of type, which, when locked up and put through the press, will multiply the original to any desired extent. Every letter, point, and intervening space has been specially reached for and fixed by a separate motion of the compositor's hand. Little by little the work is done. The cases, containing the alphabet, have the elements for all varieties of theme and shades of language. Out from these few little type-apartments have come all the words in the printed volumes, tracts, and periodicals of the world, with their untold influences for good or evil upon the millions since the art was known.

So is human character composed. The alphabet case before us is Time. The hours, minutes, and seconds are the apartments for the types, which, lifted and locked into place, shall spell our life. Every day is a new page. From the moulded moments before us, we pick up and set in order the thoughts that make our history. As a printer has the power to put together mischievous words and vicious sentences out of the same case of types from which a Bible might be composed, so has every accountable human being the power to make his own life what he will. He may make his history a police gazette or a Christly gospel, according to his copy and his choice. And as a printed page is not read by the world until finished and issued beyond revision, so is a man's life interpreted by what he is with rounded days and years — by what he expresses himself to be through crises and eras — rather than by his single promises and emotional actions. A page is locked into form by itself, and its impress is a unit, although related to pages before and after; so is a day or a year in a man's life. He can not get himself gauged by head-line Sunday lettering, double-leaded in the way of promised piety, and with the italics of tears, dollars, and amens in the sanctuary service, unless the weekday parts of the page be properly adjusted. The lower-case particulars must range in with a man's capital generalities. Christian character, to read well, must include the whole make-up of the years, the solid quadrats of unseen charity, the regular spaces of secret devotion, the points of punctuation in all the means of grace, the well-justified lines of daily duty, and all locked up in the form of square-living as prescribed in the New Testament. It is as necessary that the religious silences be observed as the religious speeches, in order that a Christian life may be an epistle read and known of all men. The hidden quadrats are as essential as the heady capitals in typing a page of poetry.

The copy before all men is the example of Jesus Christ. Out of our times we are to select and set together the impulses, thoughts, and actions that shall make us most like Him, so that as we who profess His name are read, we shall be able to show something of His spirit, His life and His work.

Christians are epistles to be read. The world reads them every day. How important that this living gospel which walks and trades and stirs about in public places should be correctly printed! Yet how many of these living epistles have been printed from battered type, from mixed fonts, on spotted paper, and in dim ink! But after all, orthodoxy is safer in the consecrated heart than in the theological library. Evangelism is an upright, open-eyed, warm-handed, advancing thing, not the flat flimsiness of a mere programme, to be written and put away on the shelf for safe keeping; it is always alive, alert and growing; it is not dead Latin, but vital mother-tongue in this country; it is not steepled in church, cadenced in ritual, or robed at the altar, so much as hearted in living people and radiated in workday duties.

So let us here and evermore show a gainsaying world the sacred printing on our hearts by letting the light in upon it through our common life. Let sinners read us rather than our books. Let us pronounce the gospel warm from loving lips, and emphasize it by an honest practice, and we shall accomplish more truly evangelical work than by sending off assorted packages of brimstone, tinder, and matches, sect-patented and prepaid from all eternity, to our heathenish neighbors. We must be in our places like the separate letters of a word, and the various words of a message, and as individuals and denominations, in living, lightning emphasis, spell out the gospel of salvation to dying men.

In a printing-office, sometimes, when a form or page is not well locked up, a type, a word, or a line drops out and spoils the meaning. The chase must be square and sound, and the quoins firm and well driven. So when a church has no definite rule of faith, and no disciplinary appliances by which to hold men together; in the looseness of doctrine and duty, men drop out from their appointed places in entire words and lines, as represented in the fellowhood of families—drop out and are *pied*, marring the significance of great congregations. It is difficult to read the meaning of a church where once-active members are missing. The blanks arrest the eye of the world before the beauties. A full pew will not begin to excite the remarks that an empty pew will excite, because these breaks and vacuums are unnatural. Some fashionable churches prefer, doubtless, to have the people adjusted in select groups and far between, richly clad and sweetly scented, in a kind of poetical measure of fours and twos, the vacant places of crimson-cushion being supposed only to give accent to the syllabled solemnity that ranges itself rhythmically across the pews, as a printer arranges short-lined but deep-thoughted poems across the middle of the page. But there is more truth than poetry in a solid page of print at last. A student in a boarding-school, on handing his composition to the teacher, was asked, "Why do you begin every line with a capital letter?" "Why, sir, that's poetry." Just as if! And to see the manner in which some pewed churches arrange their capitalists, the most successful business-men occupying the principal places — the aisle-end prominences of the sanctuary on sunny Sabbaths, with families and servants ranged down toward the corners — gives hint of the student's vain ambition, "Why, sir, this is poetry!" Just as if, again!

The gospel is fact, and not fancy. Who does not worship more profitably and blessedly in a church-room full of happy souls, with all the caste bars broken down? A type picked and gouged out of a form is ruined; but a type dropped out may be replaced and made to print as sharply as any unfallen letter in the case. But the printers call that place where castaway, broken, and battered types are collected, an awful place! So that place where wanderers, and backsliders, and beaten church-members are grouped — no more to aid in words or works of love — is hell! O, Christian, make every thing tell for truth? The end of church life is not form, not ease, not independence — but the showing of an epistle that shall be read and known of all. Job prays for the same impressiveness of life, "O that my words were now written! O that they were printed in a book!" So, evermore, as the Bible itself has come out of quiet cloisters and crumpled manuscripts, and been multiplied, published, and proclaimed abroad to the expectant millions, may it be our daily ambition and prayer, in the composition of our life which shall be read by the ages to come, to get out of creedly coverings and traditional ways, and to put by lip and by life our motive meaning before the world — to become more legible to our fellow-men!

"The deeds we do, the words we say,
Into still air they seem to fleet,
We count them ever past—
But they shall last;
In the dread judgment they
And we shall meet!"

THE WEAVER.

" I have cut off like a weaver my life." — ISAIAH xxxviii. 12.

CHAPTER X.

THE WEAVER.

IT is evident, from frequent references in the Bible, and from the general character of dress, that woven fabrics were among the earliest productions of human hands. Weaving is of even greater antiquity than spinning, the first materials combined into woven web being reeds, blades, barks, and strips of leather. These rude fibers were plaited and crossed into each other and driven into compact texture by simple machinery, and cut and seamed into various articles of clothing long before the art of making yarn from wool or hemp was known.

The Egyptians were the earliest manufacturers of linen and other cloths; and the products of their looms were eagerly sought by foreign nations. On the old monuments at Thebes, there are pictures of looms, and of weavers at work; and although the representations show the machines to have been exceedingly crude, yet it is certain that by this means many very fine specimens were manufactured. This statement is corroborated by the fact that at the present time, the Hindoos produce exquisite muslins from their rude looms, the same in construction as those used by the ancient Egyptians. On these primitive contrivances of beam, heddle and sley, as depicted on the crumbling tombs, the fine, elastic, and durable mummy-cloth was woven for the dead.

Weaving was a special employment in some of the larger towns of Greece; but in that age of the world, it was an essential item of female education to know how to weave; hence almost every dwelling had a loom at which the women worked.

The ancient Romans used every inducement to encourage domestic industry. Spinning and weaving constituted the principal occupation of the women. It was considered a better qualification for matrimony than wealth. The *atrium* was a place set apart for female industry, that their workday habits might be conspicuous. They rather invited than avoided inspection in their working apparel. But, in aftertimes, the women of rank became luxurious and lazy, and began to be ashamed of their looms; the real dignity of labor sank lower and lower, and indolence and false modesty at length so completely made slaves of women, that they would actually apologize and blush when caught with broom or brush in hand: "Excuse me, for really I did n't expect to be seen in this business; but just at this time, we are without a girl, and the awful necessity is upon me to take hold of things myself, just for a day or so. Now, you *will* excuse my appearance, won't you?"

All the while, a woman is never so beautiful and attractive as when engaged in just such work — making home pleasant. It is angel work to banish dust and gloom from earthly dwellings, and to smile and sing in ministries of love.

In the book of Proverbs, the wise man, speaking of a virtuous woman, a model of goodness and grace, of health and beauty, says: "She seeketh wool and flax, and worketh willingly with her hands. She layeth her hands to the spindle, and her hands hold the distaff. She is not afraid of the snow for her household: for all her household are clothed with scarlet. She maketh herself coverings of tapestry; her clothing is silk and purple. Her husband is known in the gates, when he sitteth among the elders of the land. She maketh fine linen and selleth it; and delivereth girdles unto the merchant. Strength and honor are her clothing; and she shall rejoice in time to come."

There are females in these days, educated in colleges and courted by bachelors of art, who would not be able, if asked, to define the meaning of the word spindle, or distaff,— who would scorn to wear anything that would excite even a lurking suspicion of having been homemade. The Bible estimate of female character makes no allowance for craziness after foreign wares, fashion and mammon to the contrary notwithstanding. The real worth of womanhood and the enduring charm of female society are most fitly expressed in those words and works which bless the home. Home is next to heaven. Woman is sister to angel. She is not a mere ornament or a toy; neither a slave nor a drudge; she was not created from his head to rule, nor from his foot to be trodden down; but from his side, to stand as sharer in domestic duties; and in social, intellectual, religious, and political privileges, his honorable equal in all ages and lands. A true woman knows how to work, and delights in being busy with hand or brain, or both; and she lives, moves, and has her being, not the more to be ministered unto than to minister. She rises early, says Solomon. She has no ball-room midnights of show and dance and dainty feasting, to make up in sunny mornings by lying in bed till noon; she puts her hand to the spinning-wheel and distaff, to the sewing-machine and broom, as proudly as her husband to his plough, or plane, or trowel. She does not consider it beneath her dignity, or an infringement upon her liberty, or a narrowing of her rights, to share in the common toils of life. It is not enough to engage in the light-fingered lace-work and gossamer-laid fancies — those infinitesimal niceties that never tax the muscles — those delicate things that are next things to nothings at all; the true woman puts her strength and soul into ordinary work in her chosen sphere, as a man does into his. These are the equal rights and the equal honors that are so beautifully inculcated in the Bible.

The days when women whirled the spinning-wheel and plied the loom in this country are not quite forgotten yet. When these lands were new, before pianos and organs were common in the parlor, there was a music of winter evenings, when the wood fire roared and the spindle hummed, and the happy mothers, spinning, sung their children into the paradise of dreams. This is an ancestral honor that many dainty dandies and befashioned maidens now would fain disown! Indeed, there are here and there in American society persons who wear nothing but imported fabrics and fanciful fixtures every day, who move in the rustle of silk and satin only, whose school-day garments were spun and woven, cut and stitched, by a skillful mother's fingers. The times have changed. But, after all, there never shall be painted a more beautiful picture than that of the bygone days, when the flax-fields, bordered round by heavy forest green, waved in purple bloom, and webs of linen bleached white as snow upon the meadow grass! The whir of the fliers and the spool when the downy flax from the distaff and the velvety rolls of wool from the yielding hand were drawn out in threads and wound away, and the beat-beat of the busy loom made as charming sound to the souls of our fathers and mothers as the tones of piano and guitar to their fastidious children and children's children now. Yes, the times have changed; but whether toward or from the Eden joys, let him who considers and discovers tell! Still, the health and bliss of honest work are very sure.

In the language of weavers, the long threads are called the *warp*, and the cross threads are called the *woof*. The warp is wound about a beam in the loom, to be unrolled as it is met by the woof and wrought into the web; while the woof is contained in the shuttle, a small, boat-like instrument, driven horizontally across the warp by the weaver's hand, from right to left, and from left to right in rapid flight.

In the book of Job, our days are compared to the weaver's shuttle, passing and repassing so very swiftly, every throw leaving a thread behind it; and when they are finished, the thread is cut off and the web taken out of the loom for inspection, measurement, and future use.

The meaning of the words, "I have cut off like a weaver my life," is, that as a weaver cuts off from his loom his finished web, and hands it, in its own weight and measurement, to the inspector, so does a man his life. For life is a web. The simile is instructive. The prophet, in his striking description of death, employs this figure of speech to make sharp impression on the mind. It implies that the middle-aged are most unwilling to die. Children are easily reconciled to death, and so are old people. They pass over into the eternal state quietly and peacefully. Death is not dreadful to them. But the man in his prime, with plans but half accomplished, and with prospects ever brightening and beckoning before him; the man with strong pulse and clear eye and dextrous hand; the man in the mid-way journey and joy of his life,—is afraid and unready for the experiment of dying. A man's most solemn words are spoken when he stands face to face with death, and especially when the summons comes in the shock of a moment, and in the midst of smile and song and highest noon of being. When the messenger announces his coming to a man in supposed security—with health and wealth enough for years of ease, and insists upon the immediate dissolution of soul and body, it cuts the thread in the work of weaving, and bears away into the judgment light the web for the Master's eye and solemn word.

The prophet shows the real power of prayer; for there are added out of heaven fifteen years to a man's life in answer to simple faith. As soon as the appeal reaches the throne of God, the sun is commanded to measure out to a fleshly mortal the exact surplus to a moment, before the grave should receive his dust. A late writer has said that this incident includes "a history, an elegy, and an anthem all in one." The thought before us might well be called a part of the elegy.

Every man is a weaver, and character is the web he weaves. Reputation is but a painting or printing of unoriginal figures on the surface; character-making is the working of new designs and combinations into the texture of the web. The one is external. The other is internal and thorough. The one fades; the other brightens by wear. Reputation washes out. Character is the more firmly set in order and brilliance by every cleansing test. The Christian is not a painter of reputation; he is a weaver of character.

In forming character there are two distinct elements, corresponding with the weaver's warp and woof. There are some things which unwind from eternity—immortal principles that emanate only in the purities of heaven. They are let down to men from above, as warp is advanced to the weaver in the loom, and as they live and work up to the giving. These divine principles are faith, hope, and charity, and their parallels. Providence arranges them in order, and adjusts them to our life, to be met and crossed into unity by works of patience, benevolence, and prayer. These celestial elements of character are like the weaver's warp, strong, lasting, and regular. They are the eternal threads which may be woofed into beauty for heavenly adornment, or marred and knotted into sackcloth palls for outcasts in darkness forever. The warp is wisely arranged by the fingers of God. The materials of the woof are lying about us awaiting the spindle, the texture, the tinting, and the weaving into whatever is appointed before us in the opening of the days. Our actions, our words, our thoughts — these are the threads we select from the circumstances about us. We wind them into the shuttles of the flying hours by our own hands, and weave them into the ever-lengthening web of character by the pulse-beats of our own hearts.

"Ceaselessly the weaver Time,
  Sitteth at his mystic loom,
Keeps his arrowy shuttle flying —
Every thread a-nears our dying —
And with melancholy chime,

Very low and sad withal,
Sings his solemn madrigal,
As he weaves our web of doom.
'Mortals!' thus he, weaving, sings,
'Bright or dark the web shall be,
As ye will it; all the tissues
Blending in harmonious issues,
Or discordant colorings;
Time the shuttle drives, but you
Give to every thread its hue,
And elect your destiny.'"

In cloth-making, both warp and woof are necessary. But the warp is always considered the superior element in the web. So in character-weaving, both faith and works are essential. Faith, the heavenly principle, is the superior element, because the gift of God; this is the strength and stay of character. But works, which are human, blend with, bind into, and make body of faith. The human will mingles with the divine will, the finite with the infinite, and things present with things to come. Results are at the choice of the weaver. No angel shapes his own character, as a man shapes his. For angels are not free agents in the sense that men are free. They are high and holy in their creation. But man has the peculiar privilege of electing his destiny as he will. This is his distinguishing prerogative. He rises by discipline, and becomes a co-worker with God in securing his own immortality. He stands upon the earth, and gathers out of its chaos and ruins, and weaves into his character by choice, what no other beings can. An angel would make miserable failures in his plan, and get forward awkwardly with man's work put into his hands. Angels would have no Christ as Redeemer, Pattern, and Guide. The looms in which man weaves character for eternity would snap the delicate fibers of seraph-life into shreds. None but mortals have such a wondrous scheme before them — a loom which moves only because the Son of God came down to earth and attached the thread of his own divine life to ours, while suns were darkened and worlds made to tremble at his tread. Immortal humanity will present designs and glories transcending the visions of archangels; for the image of Jesus will give special grace and grandeur to every saint that shines in heaven.

Materials for weaving are common to all. The world is full of helps. As communities, men may accomplish great things; they may form parties, shape republics, and give tone to the world's times; but in character-weaving every man must make his own. There is no borrowing or lending of looms; no interlapping nor exchanging of threads. No other can weave a man's character for him. We may escape the old Roman custom of a loom in every house; we may make unfashionable the primitive notions of industry; we may hire our garments done in mammoth manufactories, or import them ready-made from foreign nations, and be innocent of the very name and nature of the fabrics we wear. But every man and every woman is held to the work of weaving personal character. God does not furnish men, as angels, with characters ready-made. A man's character is his own moral and immortal self. He can not lease himself out to his party or his sect, and by contract get his weaving done against the judgment-day.

In this sense, we are God's workmanship, as

St. Paul has it. Our motives, our passions, our energies, and our influences are inherent in our creation. These are the materials from which we shape ourselves. These are furnished us to use as a weaver the flax and the wool. It is in the direction which we give to these things, the relations into which we combine them, and the use that we make of them, that we become co-workers with God. He works in us both *to* will and *to* do; but at the same time it is we, as men accountable and reasoning, who *will* and *do* ourselves; and thus we really work out, after God helps us to begin it, our own salvation. God never violates our free agency. He furnishes us the materials for substantial character, reaches our minds and consciences by arguments, and inspires us with a zeal to carry forward what he plans for our good and his own glory.

"Countless chords of heavenly music,
  Struck ere earthly time began,
Vibrate in immortal concord
  To the answering soul of man;
Countless rays of heavenly glory
  Shine through spirit pent in clay,

On the weavers at their labors —
  On the children at their play.
Man has gazed on heavenly secrets,
  Sunned himself in heavenly glow,
Seen the glory, heard the music, —
  We are greater than we know."

This life-weaving never ceases. It is not a question whether the work shall go on. No human being can stop the unwinding warp which his own heart-throbs bring down out of eternity. The only choice is whether the filling in shall be good or bad, distorted or beautiful. No weaver goes to his loom and flings an empty shuttle to and fro the whole day long. He would be a fool to ply the heddles and sling the sley without a crossing thread,— to waste his time, spend his strength, and wear out his loom for nothing. Yet such a blank task could be done. There might be such a fool. But in life there is a thread, though always a brittle thread. As long as man moves he is accountable. There is no such thing as swinging an empty shuttle. Some sort of web is weaving every hour. Our very intuitions go into the wondrous fabric, tingeing the texture of the web. There is no holiday, no respite from the continuous work. Yet the weaver need not weary, if he but put his soul with his strength into his task. If hard at first, if the shuttle drag with its fullness, and the loom start muscles into aching, still the patient weaver soon acquires skill, and by-and-by he sings as he plies the treadles, throws the shuttle, strikes the reed; for he begins to see the charming figures taking shape as a panorama of beauty under his hand. He now smiles at the soft tintings of his yesterday's tears that dropped into the warp as he wept. He sings as much as he sobs; he rejoices over as much as he regrets. The man who weaves his own will into God's will, sees angel-like images under his eyes, and while his heart beats with hope, he sings praise and toils joyfully forward in his weaving.

But, be we full of gladness or of grief, of hope or of fear, the work goes on and on forever. Sometimes the royalest patterns are outwrought in the dark, and under the beatings of sorest trouble. There was a day when Job did not know what he had in his loom.

He had lost property, friends, health, influence — every thing but life. He had nothing to weave into his web but sobbing breaths and spirit agonies. He was forsaken and heart-broken; but, poor Job! he wove in these thrums, ragged, and torn, and soiled, and thin. For there was a heavenly design in all his bereavement which did not then and there appear. God was all the while fixing the heddles to turn a magnificent picture in the web. Now, every age and all the angels admire that monotony of mourning which was woven in with tears and pain. Job himself sees now what then he was permitted to do. Who in heaven among the happy hosts can show a finer, fairer pattern than that which wrought in the potsherd and the ashes!

Christian, never mind the sorrows. Those things that are dark and rough on the earthly side of your weaving are the brightest and best on the heavenly side. You weave for immortality and not for time. The right side of your work will be unrolled before you after a while, all radiant with beauty and surprise. Sore bereavements, deaths of friends, the crape at windows and doors, the hearse that rumbled away so dismally with your darling dead, the yellow clay of the new grave, the mound of springing green that turns ashy dull in the autumn drought, — all these are brilliant on the eternal side of the weaving. The more confused and tangled the earthly side, the more rich and rare the glory of the heavenly.

> "The soul, reposing on assured relief,
> Feels herself happy amidst all her grief!
> Forgets her labor as she toils along —
> Weeps tears of joy and bursts into a song."

Weave on. Weave well. Keep the thread of life a-flying. The more you put into character here that is true and strong, the better will be your immortality. The life and truth of Christ Jesus, the influences of the Spirit, the events of common life — duties, obligations, self-denials, losses, sorrows, — do n't reject them; weave them all in. These are the weaver's wool and flax. The joys, gains, blessings, sympathies, affections — weave them in without purloining. These are the weaver's silk and silver threads. All these the Master furnishes. He bids you use them as they come. It is yours to search them out and weave them in. To one he gives less, to another more, to all a part, according to each man's capacity to appreciate and use. There must be nothing wasted, nothing refused, nothing concealed for other purpose. Life-character is a question of patience, perseverance, skill, muscle, and honor. This life-loom never stops for want of thread. The flying shuttle never strips the quill. Every weaver has his hands full, and must be wide-awake and busy-footed to keep the treadles going!

"Our many deeds, the thoughts that we have thought;
 They go out from us, thronging every hour;
 And in them all is folded up a power
 That on the earth doth move them to and fro;
And mighty are the marvels they have wrought
 In hearts we know not, and may never know."

"I have cut off like a weaver my life." There is an end. There is a last trip for the shuttle. There is death. Cloth wears out, but character does not. In the last chapter of the Bible it is said, "He that is unjust, let him be unjust still; and he that is righteous, let him be righteous still; and he that is holy, let him be holy still." At death the work is over. Then the rattling loom must stop, and the pulsing heart be still. There will be no opportunity then for overgoing bad work, adjusting awkward designs, or covering false figures. When the sley has ceased to swing, and the treadles drop upon the floor, then the shears cut off the web, and just as it is, through and through from selvage to selvage and from end to end, it is handed over to the Master. It is examined as a weaving, not as a painting. Reputation is something at a funeral; it insures long procession and eligible lot. But it is nothing in the judgment. Character, after death, is everything. Will this life-fabric — this soul-weaving — hold together in eternity? This is the grand question of all life. For the Master disposes of it exactly according to its worth.

Very soon, and nothing but our work will be left. Wealth will be gone; health will be gone; reputation will be gone; all will be gone but character. That remains forever. What have you in your loom? How are you weaving? Is the likeness of Jesus taking form, is his glory coming forth, as your thoughts go in and your pulses beat, and the circling suns go round and round?

THE DAY-LABORER.

"Man goeth forth unto his work, and to his labor, until the evening." — PSALM civ. 23.

CHAPTER XI.

THE DAY-LABORER.

GRAND is the poem from which these words are selected, and it is syllabled all through with the music of nature. It celebrates the order of God's universe, the harmony of the seasons, the beauty and bounty of the fields, trees, waters, and living creatures, with all the various phenomena of the material world.

Among the distinct statements concerning the economies which God has instituted, we find this verse of Scripture: "Man goeth forth unto his work, and to his labor, until the evening." It teaches that the Creator's plan of worlds implies human industry. The word man, here, is general; it includes all men and all women — the aggregate of humanity; it associates labor with every individual of the race. Daily work is announced as a settled fact in the arrangement of nature, and sung as a pæan of praise to the Lord. The will of Heaven toward men is that they should have regular employment. Labor is as necessary and as dignified as the revolving of the sun in his circuit, the changing of the moon, the harvest-yield of the earth, the coursing of the waters down the valleys and among the hills, the distribution of the rain, the errands of the wind, the sweep of the tides, or any other of the movements of inanimate creation. The Psalmist puts all celestial and terrestrial operations in sublime accord with the every-day duties of men. It is as much the divine will and plan that human hands should be busy, as it is that nature should observe her appointments from the beginning until the end of time. Every created finger has its place and its work, and is, in its errands, as important in the grand summing of things, as any star that shines, or any world that yields its increase.

The Bible makes human labor a sacred ordinance, and claims a special service from every hand, as well as from every head and every heart. The gift of reason includes the obligation to work. Man's physical existence is dependent on the use of his own hands. His food and raiment are to be wrought out of crude elements by toil, tact, and patience. The beasts have matured provision for all their wants. They are fed and clothed by the Hand that created, and have ample and seasonable supplies. But man must coax the earth for his bread; he draws his comforts from reluctant sources. He must build his own shelter, weave his own garments, invent and provide his own accommodations. Nature is a storehouse of ready-made wares, free and full, for brute and bird, for fish and fowl, for insect and reptile, all the year and every where; but man must look out for himself. He is furnished with raw materials only. He must work them into supplies, or shiver and starve. Nature gives to man but hints and helps. She hides her gold deep in the mountains, her pearls deep in the sea, and says, "Now dig and dive, and you shall have them. She puts her bearded wheat and delicious fruits forward of the seedtime and the planting by tedious months and years, with storm and snow between; and the sower and the planter must wait, watching and tilling the ground until the gleaning days. Dwellings are to be delved out of the quarries, cut out of the forests; clothes are to be spun from the wool, the cotton, and the flax, and woven in the loom; all essentials and all luxuries are alike to be reached only by search and struggle and sweat; and no era shall ever dawn to change this divinely appointed method of living by labor, day by day, and century by century, while the world endures.

"No man is born into the world whose work
Is not born with him; there is always work,
And tools to work withal, for those who will;
And blessèd are the horny hands of toil."

So it is in intellectual attainments. A wealthy man, on visiting his daughter in a fashionable boarding-school a long way off,* and learning that she was behind her classes, inquired what was wrong. "Why, sir, your

* How singular that the best boarding-schools always happen to be those a long way off!

daughter has no capacity to keep her place in this school." "*Capacity!* No capacity—is *that* what she needs? Then, sir, I'll buy her one this very day!" That would be a convenient arrangement for the rich in purse and the proud in spirit who are poor in intellect. But nature preserves a broad democracy in human brains. Pockets get unbalanced and unequaled in the speculations of a day; but heads are only and always what they are made by study. Man must work for knowledge. He never wins it in a game. It is not in the markets. It is only in the mines. The lower orders of creation are furnished with a peculiar kind of knowledge—ready made—and it is packed under their skulls in a kind of predestined fixedness in the form of instinct, the same from the world's first mornings till now; but man comes into being helpless, ignorant, and slow of sense—a next thing to nothing, without any idea of his place, his wants, or his possibilities; and he would remain so during some sort of a forever, unless he were trained and strengthened into a knowledge of his nature. The scholar implies the student.

The mind is developed and disciplined only by labor. There are grandeurs, delights, and glories in mental attainment; but work—hard work—is the price that brings them into possession.

The same principle holds good in morals. There could be no saving religion without obligation, without duties to perform, trials to endure, deeds to accomplish, powers to develop, penalties to avoid, happiness to attain, a God to love, obey, and honor, and a self to grapple and subdue. Heaven is not so low a place that men may drift into it as rubbish; it is high, pure, and holy, and must be entered by flight as on eagles' wings—by faith, by working, overcoming faith.

Man glorifies himself by work. It is *man* that goeth forth to his work and to his labor; not a slave, not a menial, not a second-rate biped in the shape of a man; but man himself. He takes his manhood into his toil, and adds to his manhood by his toil. The word man has a clearer ring than gentleman. When man becomes too gentle to work, he is too gentle to be a man; he is less and meaner than man. The Bible talks about men, and not about gentlemen. Gentleness may be becoming in a dove or a sheep; but a man is the nobler for nerve, courage, grit,—for muscle, for brawniness, tan, bronze, bone, blood, brain, knuckle, knot; he must have breadth and strength and solid build of body. Man is himself fearfully and wonderfully made—made for a purpose, for positive power, for daily work. He has the planning intellect and the executive hand to match; he has ambition and affection, like the tides of a mighty sea, pressing all his powers into action. He is unmanned and begins to fall into ruin the moment he ceases to work. A man with nothing to do is as unsightly and pitiable as Nebuchadnezzar at grass alongside of the oxen in the field.

What wonders man has done! He has changed the face of the world. He has leveled mountains and exalted valleys, harnessed the winds to his commerce, seized and trained the lightnings into obedient messengers, bound continents together in iron bands, established nations, built cities, turned deserts into gardens, and made the wild elements bow at his bidding.

It is only by activity that man can understand himself and develop his powers. From the beginning the command has been, "Till the earth, and keep it." In the days of Adam's innocence he was required to work. It was a condition in the enjoyment of earthly paradise. God speaks to all classes and orders of humanity — to rich and to poor in equal emphasis — "Six days shalt thou labor and do all thy work." After this direct teaching, seeing that the whole order of our being is involved in our responsiveness to the demands of labor, it is clear, that, *not to work is morally wrong.* It is a violation of the rules by which the universe is governed. All men are appointed to labor; and to disobey or to neglect is rebellion against heaven. Laziness is a sin, as positive and punishable as theft, robbery, or murder. God says, "Thou shalt not steal;" and in the same decalogue, with equal emphasis, he says, "Six days *shalt* thou labor." If the obligation to work is limited to a class, so may a class claim that it is not crime for them to kill and steal. If one man can be honorably excused from labor, the very same reasoning will excuse and make honorable the cutting of a neighbor's throat for his money. These "shalts" and "shalt nots" on the tables of stone are the Almighty's words, and demand attention. There is not a superfluous letter in the Decalogue. There is not a tone or syllable in the Sinai thunders intended for rhetorical effect. There is no escape from daily work by any maneuver of interpretation. You may profess to be religious; commit to memory the commandments, and recite them with angel eloquence; build churches with spires to pierce the clouds; attend service every Sabbath, rain or shine; hear sermons; make prayers; sing praises; support the gospel, — you may be orthodox to the shading of the last period in your book of faith, and evangelical to the measure of sobs and tears toward the heathen; but if, after all, as individuals, you do not put your own hands to some steady work, and drive forward with your own life-powers some legitimate calling, you disobey the plain command of God, and are held in stricter accountability than a pagan or a cannibal. Lounging is sinning. Mere sentiment in Christianity is miserable heresy. Indolence, where there are brain, heart, and hand to be engaged, is outright crime. In the grand economy of worlds and souls, it is the Divine plan that man shall go "forth to his work and to his labor, until the evening."

Inaction is injurious to the physical being. The body needs the perpetual exercise of work. The mind needs the constant stimulus of thought. The heart needs the ceaseless impulses of hope and expectation. You find neither brightest intellect, healthfulest form, nor happiest spirit under the feathers of fashion. There may be tinsel and glitter and elegance without, but it is assumed; it is put on for effect; it is but the thin borrowal from books; it is artificial, and fades with the breaths of the passing hour. Robustness, vigor, grace, symmetry of body, force of character, real personality, and genuine charm of life are found only by the ways of every-day work. The medicine-takers, the grumblers, the whimsical women, the moping, melancholy men, the delicate young people who dare not venture out in the rain, or sun, or snow, or storm, the feeble mothers, the insipid fathers, — the world's whole motley herd of unhappy and invalid people, are generally the idle and inactive — the gentlemen and ladies of society. The wholesome bodies, the ruddy cheeks, the happy souls are found among the laboring masses. They who go forth in the morning to their work and to their labor move in the order and share the dignity of stars that shine in the firmament, and of crystal waters that dance and sing among the hills. The laws of true living demand a regular occupation for head, and heart, and hand.

Not only is indolence self-abusive, but it injures others. It makes a man a sponge. The idler lives on the efforts of others. He is a thief. All want, all hunger, all nakedness, all ordinary physical suffering, may be traced to the delinquency of hands which God made for work. In the judgment-day there will be a fearful reckoning against soft, white hands, as well as against hard, black hearts.

Labor is not to be estimated as drudgery.

If equally divided and promptly done, it would give sweetest rest and amplest reward. "Man goeth forth unto his work and his labor, *until* the evening." The day is work-time, as a general rule. No man is to drag his service into the dark hours of the night. The day in which he begins, must, in its evening, furnish him release, reward, and rest. There is a proper time with limit to labor. "Six *days*," shalt thou labor; not six days and nights, and Sunday, too! Day-laborers are overtaxed. Employers would get more work done, and better done, by exacting less time. Who that toils from twelve to fifteen hours each day, can claim an evening as his own? *Until* the evening means into the midnight, too often.

Because of the fashions and follies of many, others are compelled to sacrifice health and home-comforts to the cruelty of overwork. There are mothers, sisters, and wives in Christendom, wearing their lives away under relentless bondage. In dark alleys, in narrow rooms, with scanty clothing and unwholesome fare, without social recognition or sympathy, unknown, patient and uncomplaining, there are some of God's poor spending their days in drudgery, awaiting the release of death. And this pinching poverty comes of the extravagance of the rich,—for wherever there is overindulgence in one direction, there are overwork and distress in another. It is because some men and some women do nothing at all, that others are made to bear such heavy burdens; and so both the idle and the overworked are prematurely old in spirit and broken in body. There is a dreadful responsibility resting upon the fashionable portion of the community who despise work and grudge the laborer his bread.

"'Go till the ground,' said God to man,
'Subdue the earth, it shall be thine;'
How grand, how glorious was the plan!
How wise the law divine!
And none of Adam's race can draw
A title, save beneath this law,
To hold the world in trust.
Earth is the Lord's, and he hath sworn,
That ere old Time has reached his bourn,
It shall reward the just!"

Some people draw a line between religion

and common work; they imagine a broad gulf between this life and the life to come. They fancy that worldly employments are misfortunes of the fall and hindrances to spiritual life. They think that, if only they could escape labor, they could elude the devil and make sure advance toward heaven. This notion arises from the false teaching of that theology that would reduce Christianity to mere doctrine, tone, way, and professionality.

We must study Christ and his gospel on the uncumbered page of inspiration for ourselves. We shall see that God places all his creatures in the best possible training-schools for higher life. He does not bewilder men with theories, nor tantalize them with conditions which they may not easily accept. The caterpillar is exactly adapted to the future career of a moth: and the chrysalis is best conditioned in its dumb helplessness to the coming glory of the butterfly. Infancy is the easiest and most graceful introduction to childhood; and childhood laughs and leaps with shout and spring into muscular manhood. The analogy holds good in reference to our immortality. It is by the necessities put upon us for work, and by our very struggles forward and upward, that we get from shell to wing, and attain the heights of the heavenly kingdom. David, when a shepherd, with crook and harp and sling, was training for kinghood over men, and out on the grassy sunlit hills he qualified himself for his scepter and his crown. Peter, and Andrew, his brother, by fishing in Galilee, acquired the skill to catch men in the gospel net. Seining the sea toughened them into courageous apostleship. Yet a shepherd lad in the fields would hardly have been selected by worldly-wise men as the rising ruler of the Hebrew nation; nor the plodding fishermen, amidst the slime and scale and smell of their seines, pointed out as eloquent apostles of the world's Messiah. No one can prophesy what a Christian laboring man may become in the kingdom of heaven. For it doth not yet appear what he shall be. Hugh Miller, the workday schoolmaster, says that one of the best persons he ever knew, and his acquaintanceship was large and royal, was a poor widow of Inverness, in Scotland,—a woman who was always patient, always busy, always happy, always content. "She was an humble washerwoman," he remarks, "but I am convinced that in the other world, which she must have entered long ere now, she ranks considerably higher." The example of Christ, the carpenter, constantly presents itself before the day-laborer, as a motive of commanding power. For there is something grand and satisfying above us which can be attained unto only by way of toil, tears, and spended strength; but it is well worth the cost, and comes into the possession of every soul made weary and worthy by the strife.

> "In the world's great harvest-day,
> Every grain, on every ground —
> Stony, thorny, by the way —
> Shall a hundred-fold be found."

When Satan comes to tempt any soul, it is a hero-heart that makes itself bound with the bliss of telling him to his face: I am not at leisure to listen to your propositions. I am otherwise employed. I am in the service of God and of my fellow souls; my work is lawful and joyous; my thoughts nor my energies are in the market for bidders. *I have a permanent situation with Christ Jesus.* Such a speech would move the devil to confusion and retreat. But some professed Christians are so persistently idle and worthless — so vacillating, restless, and inquisitive, that they even *tempt the tempter to tempt them;* and it is no wonder that they are utterly undone at last. They have deliberately crossed the enemy's lines and put themselves in his grasp. They have played with adders and scorpions as pastime, and been bitten for eternity.

> "Man walks in a vain show:
> He knows, yet will not know;
> Sits still when he should go;
> But runs for shadows: —
> While he might taste and know
> The living streams that flow,
> And crop the flowers that grow
> In Christ's sweet meadows."

An old poet represented Pluto to be the god of riches and of hell, — as if hell and riches were under one jurisdiction! The deity so pictured was lame, yet fleet as fire or the wind. When Jupiter sent him to a soldier or a scholar, he went limping, but when to a fool or a harlot, he went like lightning. The moral is plain, and applies in Christendom to-day. The riches that come from God and to honest men, come slowly; but the riches that come by unjust dealing and fraud, flow in like lava from a belching volcano. The man who throws aside religion, and opens all his soul for gold, and grabs after wealth as a wrecker for spoils, may soon be rich. When the spring of conscience is screwed up to the highest pin that can be touched without breaking; when Christianity is frowned outside the exchange, the office, and the store, and locked up as a prisoner in the somber sanctuary all week long, and forbidden on pain of excommunication to look into private business transactions, then the devil is on his throne. For he will rush a man into hell in a cushioned chariot as willingly as drag him there through the gutters on his back. But the honest, busy day-laborer acquires vigilance, builds granite character upon sure foundations, appreciates and enjoys his slow but steady gains, and is overmatch for the cunning Destroyer. He has taken religion into his heart, and it now courses in his blood, — it makes bone, fiber, muscle; it permeates and purifies his inmost being, and serves the Lord through soul and body, which is the most reasonable service. Such a man works as if he believed.

"*Until the evening!*" Every day has its special duties, and they must be done in their day. Every morning should find men up and doing. The sunlight is kindled for work, and not for show or idle play. The birds sing welcomes to the dawning day, brushing in diamond drops the dew from bough and twig in the tremble of their throbbing melodies. The flowers are sweetest and fairest in the morning, the sunshine cheeriest, the air purest and clearest of all the day. Nature is eloquent in invitations to labor. The most delicious daily bread is daily earned. "Give us, *this day*, our daily bread." A modern Christian economist, the head of some wholesale establishment, would amend this petition by praying, "Give us, *this year*, our daily bread," and make the one asking do for a thousand eatings, and call it a stroke of business! Any thing to escape the thought of daily obligation, daily need, daily duty, and daily service! "Yes, yes," the retired merchant or manufacturer may say to himself in his easy chair, "It is well enough for those poor people who live from hand to mouth to go regularly to church and to say their prayers—they need the comforts of religion; but as for me, the place is too dull and the society too common. I'm ahead of the Lord, now, for a good living these many years to come. Heaven owes me a premium for my credit at the banks, for my investment in steeples, missions, and Bibles, and for my patronage of the obscure Christ in the sunny Sabbath morning service."

Nothing can destroy selfishness but the gospel. Political reform—even the most impartial suffrage—will not make the love of neighbor equal to the love of self. Unsanctified political power may only robe and crown a moral demon in a nation's heart. Not only intelligence, but affection must have the ballot. Science, law, art, literature—all these things have been tried a thousand times, and have as often failed to reach and change the heart and control its carnal nature. The gospel only—the gospel of labor and love, of equal rights and universal brotherhood—goes to the motive centers of the soul, and saves men in their bodies and their spirits, which are the Lord's. The gospel—not our theories about the gospel; the truth—not our interpretations of the truth; the Christ—not the garbs in which we clothe him for introduction to our invited guests,—the living Christ, the people's delivering Lord, the poor man's sympathizing Friend—He is the power to "cast down every imagination and every high thing that exalteth itself against the knowledge of God."

The world wants a new translation of the gospel; not into letters, but rather into men's lives, into daily experience—made radiant in countenances, warm in deeds,—a translation that will beam forth in beatitude and benediction wherever Christians move and breathe. Rowland Hill used to say that he would give very little for the religion of a man whose very dog and cat were not the better for it.

The church wants more open-faced and ready-handed religion, and fewer gossiping, slandering, grumbling, gluttonous, fretful, conceited bigots as gospel representatives, especially in such a thinking, active age as this.

We little heed Isaiah's wondrous words, "Lift up thy voice like a trumpet." Voice is a great thing in religion, but it is not every thing. Boisterous prayers and exhortations are common enough. Men will sing themselves hoarse in times of revival who move never an inch in search of Christ's suffering poor. Why does Isaiah say, "Lift up thy voice like a trumpet?" There are many things that sound louder than a trumpet. The roaring of the sea is louder. The pealing of thunder is deeper. The wails of the tempest are bolder. Yet the prophet does not say, "Lift up thy voice like the sea;" or, "Lift up thy voice like the thunder;" or, "Lift up thy voice like the tempest." Why does he say as a *trumpet?* Because a trumpeter, when he sounds his trumpet, fills its throat with his breath, *and holds it up with his hand.* Voice and arm are both engaged. It is word and work in the trumpet-blast. And so every Christian is a trumpeter, going forth daily to proclaim the gospel of God. He must not merely report with his mouth, but support with his hand. His profession must be sustained by his practice. The tongue is the advocate and the hand is the executor of God's will; and when a man both speaks and works in religion, then does he lift up his voice like a trumpet. If the churches of Christ would thus sound forth the glad tidings, the remotest islands of the sea and the interiors of idolatrous continents would hear the music of millennial glory, and nations would be born in a day!

"UNTIL THE EVENING." I have read some where of a beautiful custom among the Swiss mountaineers. The Alpine herdsmen employ the echoing horn, not merely as a call to their flocks, but also for a religious service. As soon as the sun has disappeared in the valleys, and his last lingering rays are glimmering and glancing upon the snowy summits of the mountains, the shepherd who dwells in the loftiest pasture takes his horn and trumpets forth, "Praise God the Lord!" All the herdsmen on the neighboring cliffs take their horns and repeat the words, "Praise God the Lord!" This is continued for several minutes, while on all sides, as the shades of evening deepen, the mountains echo the name of God — the — Lord! A solemn stillness follows. Every man, woman, and child is on bended knee in secret prayer as the stars beam out in benediction on the Switzers' homes and hearts. By this time it is dark. The night has fully come. "Good night!" trumpets forth the herdsman on the loftiest summit. "Good night!" is repeated from all the mountain-slopes below. Then the shepherds and all their flocks are at rest, and universal peace prevails.

Thus may the shepherds on Zion's holy mountains say, as Time's evening shadows gather round, and the weary worker's work is done, "Praise God the Lord!" "Good night! *good* night!"

So he giveth his beloved sleep, and joy cometh in the morning. Yes, GOOD NIGHT!

INDEX.

INDEX.

ASSOCIATION and Communion, 43.
Arguments in Storms, 44.
A Refuge Needed, 53.
Ancient Bricks, 59.
Arduous Toil in Brickmaking, 59.
Asiatic Architecture, 63.
Avariciousness, 70.
Alloy in Human Nature, 94.
At White Heat, 100.
Air an Obstacle, 102.
All or None, 104.
A Common Metaphor, 138.
Adam — Clay, 139.
Assyrian Potteries, 139.
Ancient Vases, 142.
Aztec Monuments, 143.
Acrostical Book, An, 145.
Anthem of Minor Chords, An, 146.
All Things are the Christian's, 148.
Apathetic Churches, 153.
Arab Women's Mirrors, 171.
As in a Glass Darkly, 174.
Animals and the Gospel, 176.
Annealing Process, The, 181.
Accident on the Ohio, 199.
Angel Pilot, The, 201.
Aimless Lives, 203.
Alexandrian Library, 221.
Ancient Libraries, 221.
Art of Printing, 233.
Alpine Herdsman's Horn, 289.

BUILDING, The Church, A, 33.
Bethel, 35.
Breadth of Foundation, 41.
Babylonian Bricks, 59.
Bond or Free, 70.
Breaking Bonds, 70.
Building Character, 71.
Beginning Right, 76.
Bible Object-Lessons, 81.
Business Men, 92.
Blasting, 94.
Blowing Out, 102.
But One Model, 104.
Bible Science, 113.

Babylonian Clay-Work, 140.
Bible Proofs in Pagan Temples, 141.
But One Master, 150.
Backsliding and Renewal, 154.
Bible Glass, 171.
Bible and Science, The, 173.
Beauty out of Rubbish, 178.
Brittle Converts, 182.
Believer's Compass, The, 202.
Block-page Printing, 223.
Block-print Books, 224.
Benjamin Franklin, 230.
Blanks, 238.
Backsliders, 239.
Brevity of Life, 250.
Beginnings of Apostleship, 281.
Bargaining for Grace, 286.

CREATOR and Redeemer One, 10.
Carpenter, The Young, 13.
Convenient Revivals, 22.
Christianity Makes Common Interests, 27.
Christ the Rock, 38.
Condescension, 39.
Church Greater than Sect, 40.
Church a Home, The, 42.
Church a Lighthouse, The, 50.
Courageous Builders, 51.
Church and the Mills, The, 89.
Capitalists, 91.
Carnal Pulse-Beats, 98.
Christianity Alloyed with Mammon, 98.
Christian Work Incessant, 102.
Creed Changes — Christ the Same Forever, 105.
Christians Chilled into Sectarians, 105.
Christ's Church, 105.
Canons Become Cannons, 106.
Carpet-loom, The, 111.
Cain-craft Chronology, 114.
Compensation, 120.
Combined Forces, 121.
Chaos and Cosmos, 126.
Christianity Triumphant, 132.
Chinese Earthenware, 143.
Crosses and Conflicts, 148.
Conscience Brokers, 150.
Customers Instead of Christians, 152.
Clay in the Potter's Hands, 155.
Clay Coffins, 164.
Crystal Christianity, 180.
Christian Growth, 182.
Christian Activity, 185.
Chinese Civilization, 193.
Chinese Immigration, 195.
Christ a Pilot, 202.
Conscience a Signal-bell, 206.
Copperplate Printing, 223.
Chinese Alphabet, The, 223.
Cast-metal Types, 225.
Composition of Character, 234.
Character a Weaving, 252.
Ceaseless Labor, 259.

DIVINITY of Christ, 10, 38.
Dignity of Labor, 14, 245, 268, 282.
Divine Democracy, 24.
Duty always Noble, 25.
Destructionism *versus* Denominationalism, 44.
Divine Temple, The, 73.
Dangers of Temporal Prosperity, 97.
Divine Skill, 112.

Darwinian Development Theory, 114.
Doing as Honorable as Thinking, 128.
Days of Desolation, 147.
Denominationalism, 44, 152.
Delight or Drudgery in Work, 197.
Definition of Printing, 222.
Distinguished Printers, 231.
Deterioration of American Society, 248.
Dignity of Human Life, 258.
Death and Judgment, 263.
Day-time for Work, 285.

EVERY-DAY Religion, 23, 206, 284.
Ecclesiastical Independence, 43.
Eddystone Lighthouse, 48.
Earliest Brickmaking, 57.
Egypt, The Devil's, 68.
Educational Symmetry, 71.
Early Experiments in Metals, 84.
Egyptian Bronze, 85.
Evidences of Supreme Intelligence, 113.
Early Triumphs of Art, 118.
Economy of Labor, 120.
Ecclesiastical Egotism, 145.
Empty Forms, 151.
Earthen Pitchers, 151.
Eddy-drops, 157.
Early Writing Facilities, 220.
Epistolary Correspondence, 221.
Engraving, Art of, 222.
Evangelism, 236.
Egyptian Weavers, 243.
Equal Rights, 248.
Elements of Character, 252.

FALSE Methods, 22.
Fact the Corner-stone, 34.
Foundation of the Church, 35.
Fellowship, 44.
False Prophets, 49.
From Tent-life to Citizenship, 57.
Fire-Brick, 61.
From Acorn to Oak, 76.
First Principles in Founding, 82.
Founding a Gradual Invention, 86.
Finished Creation, The, 124.
Full Salvation, 133.
Free Salvation, 158.
Female Self-denial, 172.
Fervency in Business, 197.
Fog-bell, The, 207.
First Printing in Europe, 224.
First Adjustible Wooden Types, 227.
Faust, 228.
First Printing-Press in America, 229.
First American Newspaper, 230.
Fashionable Churches, 238.
First Woven Fabrics, 243.
Female Industry, 247.
Faith and Works, 254.
Free Agency, 255.
Future Satisfaction, 261.

GROUNDWORK Invisible, 38.
God the Builder, 45.
Grecian Ornaments, 86.
Gathering Ore, 93.
Genius and Invention, 111.
God a Worker, 112.
God a Benefactor, 125.
God a Controller, 129.

God Manifested, 130.
Glazed Coffins, 140.
Garnished Surfaces in Morals, 150.
Glass, Discovery of, 163.
Glass, Manufacture in Rome, 165.
Glass a Luxury, 165.
Glass-making in Pittsburgh, 169.
Gospel for Glassblowers, 170.
Grace through Nature, 174.
Glass, Commerce in, 178.
Glimpses Heavenward, 186.
Guttenberg, 227.
Grecian Looms, 244.
God's Workmanship, 257.
Glory of Work, The, 272.

HIDDEN Power, 11.
Humble Advent of Jesus, 12.
Holy Family, The, 13.
Human Foundations, 46.
Human Body a House, The, 72.
How to Build Manhood, 72.
Home of the Soul, 75.
Honor in the Blood, 91.
Human Ingenuity, 112.
Heralds of Christianity, 114.
Human Imperfections, 121.
Harmony, 132.
Heresy Hunters, 153.
Horace, Tribute of, to Glass, 166.
Heaven, A Present, 204.
Heavenly Pilot, The, 209.
Heavenly Invitations, 210.
Headline Reputation, 235.
Human Ability, 257.
Harmony of Nature, 267.
Health and Industry, 277.
Human Sponges, 277.
Honest Riches, 284.

INFLUENCE of Industry, 15.
Infidel Assaults, 39.
Infallibility, 47.
Invincible Men, 63.
Israel in Bondage, 65.
Imagery of Ezekiel, 81.
Ironmen, 89.
Idle Mills and Idle Churches, 101.
Inventor's Joy, The, 122.
Inventor's Victory, The, 122.
Ingenuity as Displayed in Nature, 123.
Indian Mounds, 144.
Idols Crumbling Down, 154.
Impediments, 157.
Introduction of Glass to England, 167.
Introduction of Glass to the United States, 168.
Imagery of Ancient Scriptures, 173.
Ingredients of Glass, 175.
Invention of Mariner's Compass, The, 194.
Invention of Letters, 219.
Invention of Pages, 221.
Invention of Movable Types, 226.
Influence of Printing, 228.
Intelligence of Printers, 231.
Individuality, 256.
Idleness a Sin, 274.
Idleness a Snare, 283.

JEWS and Gentiles One, 51.
Jesus Only, 53.
Jerusalem as a Blast-Furnace, 95.
Jesus a Deliverer, 212.
Job's Creed, 217.
Job's Afflictions and Faith, 260.

KINGS May Come to Want, 67.
Knowledge Attainable only by Study, 271.

LOWLY and Holy, 30.
Little by Little, 74.
Law of Resemblances, The, 83.
Leeching for a Livelihood, 91.
Lamech's Wives, 115.
Lost Arts, 118.
Lost River, The, 119.
Looking-glasses, 171.
Laws of Pilotage, 192.
Living Epistles, 236.
Legible Gospel, A, 240.
Life a Web, 250.
Looms of Life, The, 255.
Light and Dark in a Day, 259.
Labor a Condition of Life, 268.
Living Orthodoxy, 287.

MECHANIC of Nazareth, 16.
Matrimonial Problem, 27.
Making and Mending, 27.
Masonry in Architecture, 35.
Method in Salvation, 37.
Mental Masonry, 37.
Ministerial Monopoly, 40.
Mystic Masons of the Sea, 75.
Metals of Britain, 87.
Mills and Foundries in Pittsburgh, 88.
Men as Rubbish, 95.
Men Warmed and Worked, 100.
Means and Ends, 106.
Mechanism, 116.
Man a Creature, 124.
Man a Creator, 125.
Men as Moons, 127.
Miracles, 129.
Making gods for Market, 142.
Mariner's Compass, 192.
Many Books, 229.
Mummy-Cloth, 244.
Materials for Life-weaving, 261.
Mental Capacity, 271.
Moral Obligation, 272.
Man's Achievements, 273.

NEW and Old, 33.
No Clans in Christianity, 40.
No National Church, 41.
Necessity of Organization, 42.
New Jerusalem Currency, 149.
No Monopoly of Truth, 150.
Ninth of Romans, 155.
No Unsavable Humanity, 158.
Need of a Guide, 199.
Necessity for an Alphabet, 225.
Not Now, 260.
Necessity of Labor, 270.

ORTHODOXY of Work, 19.
Outdoor Devotion, 26.
Origin of Reforms, 29.
Opinions as Theologies, 45.
Out of Bondage, 63.
Old Things New Again, 118.
Oldest of Arts, 137.
Origin of Methodism, 144.
Our Destiny What we Make it, 159.
Object of Life, 205.
Orthodoxy, 236.
Outs, 237
Orthodoxy Safest with Working-people, 276.
Overwork, 279.

PERSONAL Creator, A, 9.
Patience in Evangelism, 21.
Peter the Great, 24.
Prejudice Against Labor, 28.
Preaching Through Nature, 28.
Peter or Jesus, 47.
Plains of Shinar, 57.
Poetry of Paganism, 64.
Pharaoh's Tyranny, 66.
Prophet on Iron, The, 82.
Pittsburgh the "Iron City," 87.
Philosophies Tested, 96.
Preparation for the Gospel, 103.
Progression Backwards, 115.
Primitive Architecture, 115.
Prophetic Pictures, 128.
Potter's Wheel, The, 142.
Pottery a Universal Art, 143.
Potteries of England, 144.
Poetic Imagery of Jeremiah, 146.
Par, Premium, and Discount, 147.
Plaster-of-Paris Religion, 151.
Protestant Idols, 151.
Potter's Work, 152.
Pittsburgh, First Glass Manufacture in, 169.
Patmos Visions, 185.
Pilot of Lake Erie, The, 211.
Pilots Piloted, 213.
Promulgation of Divine Truth, 218.
Pre-alphabetic Letters, 219.
Printing in Mexico, 230.
Printer's Case, 232.
Pages of Life, 234.
Punctuated Christianity, 235.
Poetical Piety, 238.
Picture of By-gone Days, 249.
Power of Prayer, 251.
Personal Accountability, 256.
Patience and Perseverance, 262.
Power and Majesty of Life, 273.
Probation and Discipline, 280.
Plain Gospel, 287.
Profession and Practice, 288.

QUARRYING and Polishing, 45.

REGISTRIES of Masonry, 35.
Royal Fraternity, 36.
Rock of Ages, 38.
Register of Believers, 41.
Roman Bricks, 60.
Religious Intolerance, 83.
Roman Art, 87.
Refiner's Fire, 96.
Reinventions, 117.
Ruins of Inventions, 126.
Redemption Accomplished, 132.
Relics of Earliest Days, 137.
Roman Antiquities, 142.
Royal Occupation, A, 167.
Religion in Remnants, 172.
Reflection from an Old Looking-glass, 173.
River Pilots, 198.
Roman Industry, 244.
Reputation and Character, 252.
Riches and Hell, The God of, 284.

SCORN for Labor Rebuked, 17.
Simplicity of the Gospel, 20.
Servant of All, The, 20.
Social Affinities, 27.
Solomon's Temple, 35.
Sectarian Chaff, 45.
Stability, 46.

Sand or Granite, 47.
Soul-Growth, 65.
Straw in Brickmaking, 66.
Slavery, 68.
Satan's Bondmen, 69.
South Sea Islands, 74.
Secular Illustrations of the Spiritual, 81.
Steps in Founding, 86.
"Strike While the Iron is Hot," 101.
Saving Strength, 120.
Steam an Evangelizer, 123.
Sect-Patents, 151.
Spiritual Potteries, 152.
Sectarian Jealousy, 153.
Spiritual Workmanship, 179.
Self-Sacrifice, 211.
Schoffer, 228.
Sound Doctrine, 237.
Solomon's Estimate of Woman, 246.
Sphere of Woman, The, 246.
Sudden Death, 251.
Selfishness, 286.
Shepherds of Zion, 290.

TRADITION of Jesus, A, 14.
Tried Stone, The, 39.
Truth Impregnable, 40.
True Church, The, 40, 179.
Temple, Divine, The, 52.
Tower of Babel, 58.
Tried as by Fire, 62.
Tubal Cain's Inventions, 116
Terra-Cotta Libraries, 139.
Terra-Cotta Tiles, 141.
Tallying Testimonies, 141
Tests of Discipleship, 149.
Theology Necessarily Fragmentary, 157.
Touch-me-nots, 183.
Tests of Usefulness, 184.
Trades' Unions, 192.
Tyrian Navigation, 196.
Tyrian Ships, 196.
Time a Weaver, 253.
Time for Labor, 278.
Tempting the Tempter, 283.

UNITY of Effort, 36.
Unity in Variety, 37, 107, 176.
Universal Welcome, 54.
Universe a Machine, The, 124.
Universal Brotherhood, 150.
Utility of the Mariner's Compass, 195.
Underwork, 279.

VARIOUSLY Colored Bricks, 60.
Variety in Unity, 37, 107, 176.
Voyage of Life, 200.
Vital Religion, 237.
Voice and Hand, 288.

WINDING-Stair, The, 64.
Works of the Coral, 74.
Workday Analogies, 82.
Workingmen, 90.
Worldly-mindedness, 99.
Wholesome Bitters, 149.
Whom He Will and Whosoever Will, 156.
Window-Glass, The First, 167.
World a Workshop, The, 175.
Woman's Work, 245.

Woman the Equal of Man, 247.
Warp and Woof, 249.
Work a Duty, 269.
Wholesale Moralities, 286.

XYLOGRAPHIC Books, 227.

YESTERDAY, To-Day, and Forever, 23.
Youth of Jesus, 11.

ZEAL, Mistaken, 22.
Zion's Precious Sons, 145.

www.ingramcontent.com/pod-product-compliance
Lightning Source LLC
LaVergne TN
LVHW020246110826
845151LV00003B/1029

* 9 7 8 1 4 2 5 5 2 8 7 7 5 *